The Architecture of Jeremiah 1-20

Other books by William L. Holladay:

The Root Šûbh in the Old Testament, with Particular Reference to Its Usages in Covenantal Contexts

A Concise Hebrew and Aramaic Lexicon of the Old Testament

Jeremiah: Spokesman Out of Time

The Architecture of Jeremiah 1-20

William L. Holladay

Lewisburg
Bucknell University Press
London
Associated University Presses

Associated University Presses, Inc.
Cranbury, New Jersey 08512

Associated University Presses
108 New Bond Street
London W1Y OQX, England

Library of Congress Cataloging in Publication Data

Holladay, William Lee.
The architecture of Jeremiah 1-20.

Bibliography: p.
Includes index.
1. Bible. O.T. Jeremiah I-XX—Criticism, interpretation, etc. I. Title.
BS1525.2.H63 224′.2 74-204
ISBN 0-8387-1523-0

PRINTED IN THE UNITED STATES OF AMERICA

Contents

The Architecture of Jeremiah 1-20

A Note on Abbreviations and Text

This study employs the customary abbreviations: MT = Masoretic Text; LXX = Septuagint; Qr = Qere; Kt = Kethib.

The edition of the MT used in this study is *Biblia Hebraica Stuttgartensia. . .*, 8, *Liber Jeremiae* praeparavit W. Rudolph (Württembergische Bibelanstalt Stuttgart, 1970). I refer to the critical apparatus of this edition by the abbreviation *BHS*. It differs considerably from its predecessor in *Biblia Hebraica*. . .editio tertia (Privilegierte Württembergische Bibelanstalt, 1950); in this third edition the critical apparatus for the book of Jeremiah was also prepared by Rudolph, in 1931.

Introduction

a. The Problem

HOW did the book of Jeremiah come to be? We are still far from understanding the way by which earlier collections of Jeremianic material were built up to become our present book of Jeremiah, in spite of all the effort expended on the problem by many scholars over a period of many decades. No real consensus has been reached, and the suggestions of individual scholars leave one with the uneasy impression that real certainty might lie forever beyond one's grasp.[1]

Scholars at work on the problem in the present century appear to have concentrated on two related issues and to have bypassed a third related issue. The two issues on which work has been concentrated are (1) the attempt to identify the contents of the *Urrolle,* that first scroll dictated by Jeremiah to Baruch, according to the account in Jer. 36, and (2) the detection of a variety of literary styles within the book (thus Sigmund

Mowinckel's "A"—the poetic oracles, "B"—the biographical material, and "C"—the repetitive sermonic material, which is couched in a style that often seems Deuteronomistic).[2]

Those who investigate the first issue often involve themselves in a particular theory of chronology: the scroll, we know (36:1), was dictated in the fourth year of Jehoiakim, and it is assumed therefore to have contained material from both Jehoiakim's and Josiah's reigns; so one makes a search for these, some kind of reasonable choice of oracles (reasonable, that is, to the scholar making the search) that would fit these requirements.[3] Those, too, who investigate the second issue are led to assumptions about the *ipsissima verba* of Jeremiah, since it is taken for granted by a good many scholars that (at least some of) the poetic oracles (the "A" material) are original to Jeremiah, while the other stylistic corpora ("B" and "C") are the work of Baruch or of some other editor—though it is to be noted that there is no complete unanimity even on this question: Otto Eissfeldt, among others, opts for "C" as the material contained in the original scroll.[4] Still other commentators are content to leave the whole question of the identity of the scroll open.[5] Recently Claus Rietzschel[6] has tried to isolate the scroll by working "from the other direction," so to speak, stripping away, layer by layer, what he considers to be later accretions; but again, his efforts may not be altogether convincing to others.[7]

The related issue that everyone seems to have bypassed is the simple matter of *outlining* the book of Jeremiah; no one has shown much interest in this matter. It is, of course, by one's outline that one displays his conception of the way the book is put together, and a lack of interest in outlining the book betrays the common assumption that such an activity would not serve any useful purpose. Admittedly, a commentary has to offer *some* kind of outline of a biblical book in order to organize the material, but the outlines that are available in current commentaries are really nonoutlines, atomistic in their approach and thus nonsignificant in their implications. The two most recent, substantial, English-language commentaries on Jeremiah (those of Hyatt and Bright) outline the first twenty chapters piecemeal (Hyatt, 14 subdivisions; Bright, 17) with vague titles like "Parables and Warnings" (Hyatt for chapter 13), "Miscellaneous Material" (Hyatt for chapter 17), and "Oracles and Confessions in Poetry and Prose" (Bright for 15:5-16:21). The two most recent, substantial, German-language commentaries (those of Rudolph and Weiser) divide the material of chapters 1-20 into two parts, at the end of chapter 6 (Rudolph assuming a chronological division between these two blocks—chapters 1-6 "from Josiah's time," chapters 7-20 "mostly from Jehoiakim's time"), but within these two large blocks Rudolph also proceeds atomistically (one oracle, or two or three oracles grouped together, at a time) and Weiser proceeds simply chapter by chapter. John Bright gives the impression of giving up before making a start:

> What makes these books [*i.e.*, the prophetic books] particularly, and one might say needlessly, difficult is the very manner of their arrangement—or, to be more accurate, their apparent lack of arrangement. . . . All seems confusion. . . . The impression [that the reader] gains is one of extreme disarray; one can scarcely blame him for concluding that he is reading a hopeless hodgepodge thrown together without any discernible principle of arrangement at all.[8]

And again,

> [Mowinckcl's literary types A, B, and C] do not, however, furnish any key to [the book's] arrangement, but rather add

> to its chaotic appearance, for the book is certainly not arranged according to its literary types. On the contrary, these are found commingled through its various parts in what can only be called a grand disarray.[9]

Basic to all these assumptions, of course, is the postulate that the only dependable unit for literary analysis is the isolated oracle, and that these oracles have been collected in some way not amenable to conclusive analysis. One hears from time to time, in analyses of prophetic material, of "key words" or "catchwords" (Stichwörter),[10] but I do not know of any effort up to the present time to work out the structure of Jeremianic poetic material on the basis of catchword links or of any other rhetorical feature.

I submit that all this tissue of assumptions can and should be challenged: the assumption that we must look at the poetic collections atomistically; the assumption that because there is no coherent chronological or topical or other obvious patterning to the material, we are therefore driven to assume chaos. These assumptions may be challenged quite simply, I think, if one backs away and enters upon another line of reasoning, somewhat as follows.

Jeremiah, we are told (and there is no reason to doubt the narrative in chapter 36), dictated a scroll to Baruch—indeed, dictated it twice, the second time with additions. One may assume that the scroll has some scope ("all the words which I have spoken to you," v. 2)—that is, that it consisted not merely of a small handful of oracles, but of a good deal more. Now, if Jeremiah was able to dictate a scroll of some scope, and twice over, then it had some shape in his mind; he did not pull oracles out at random, like marbles from a bag. Poets in an oral culture do not function this way; they must have the mnemonic, rhetorical means to retain and transmit a total corpus—and the more so if, as in Jeremiah's case, the words to be dictated are understood to be words from Yahweh, and therefore in no way to be neglected or lost.

Now Baruch, for his part, was a scribe, trained in a scribal school;[11] that is to say, he was accustomed to orderly work. One would not expect him, then, to randomize what Jeremiah had dictated, either then or later. I shall not insist at the outset that the collection of Jeremianic material that Baruch passed on to later generations was formed around the backbone of Jeremiah's dictated scroll (though it would be altogether reasonable to assume that it did); this assumption is not crucial to my argument. I simply suggest that it is difficult to imagine how any Jeremianic corpus could have left Baruch's hand in utter disarray. It must have had some kind of *shape;* both Jeremiah and Baruch, each in his own way, would have produced collections of materials that manifested *structure.*

The question then becomes: is it conceivable that any series of later editors would have so randomized the material as to have effaced altogether the shape of those earliest collections? It seems worthwhile to posit a negative answer to this rhetorical question, and thus to work through the material of the first twenty chapters of the book of Jeremiah (where the earliest collection is, or collections are, likely to be found) with a sense of expectation that some kind of shape will emerge. The present study is the result of that quest.

As a matter of fact, we must admit that we simply have not had our eyes open sufficiently to the possibility of clues to the architecture of the book of Jeremiah across a distance of several chapters. A signal example is the parallel between 1:5 and 20:14-18. Now, it is obvious that the final "confessional" passage in chapter 20 picks up the themes and words of 1:5, the initial verse of the call of Jeremiah (*mereḥem yaṣa'ti* 20:18, *teṣe' mereḥem* 1:15; and the general theme of birth employed in the whole of the passage in chapter 20). One may easily see that the intention of Jeremiah in the passage in chapter 20 is to curse his call; but should we not go on to see the verbal parallel of 20:18 with 1:5 as a great *inclusio* for the beginning and the end of the first twenty chapters?[12]

As has already been implied, there is no coherent corpus of recent literature on the question dealt with in the present study. One sees from time to time studies like that of T. R. Hobbs, "Some Remarks on the Structure and Composition of the Book of Jeremiah," *Catholic Biblical Quarterly* 34 (1972): 257-75, but this study remains to a large degree a review of the present state of the problem and a preliminary effort to isolate the large collections or blocks of material within the book. One must admit that structural studies are "in the air" at the moment, and one suspects that the next generation of biblical studies will move systematically in this direction. One indication that these questions are beginning to be raised is afforded by three essays presented at the Uppsala Congress of the International Society for the Study of the Old Testament in 1971.[13] The essays are: Meir Weiss, "Die Methode der 'Total-Interpretation,' " Paul Beauchamp, "L'analyse structural et l'exégèse biblique," and Robert C. Culley, "Some Comments on Structural Analysis and Biblical Studies,"[14] but all three of these studies are heavily theoretical, and only one offers any illustrative material.[15]

I shall therefore simply offer here a few suggestions of studies and personal conversations that have helped to stimulate my own thinking as I entered upon the present study.

One of the best examples of which I am aware of this kind of work is Edwin M. Good's study, "The Composition of Hosea" (*Svensk Exegetisk Årsbok* 31 [1966]: 21-63), in which he attempts to "make sense" out of the overall structure of that book—and, I believe, with real success.

Georg Braulik, O. S. B., has been working out structures to be found in the prose of Deuteronomy; an example of his work is "Aufbrechen von geprägten Wortverbindungen und Zusammenfassen von stereotypen Ausdrücken in der alttestamentlichen Kunstprosa," *Semitics* 1 (1970): 7-11.

I have benefited greatly from personal conversations and correspondence through the years with Dr. Jack R. Lundbom, whose dissertation, *Jeremiah: A Study in Ancient Hebrew Rhetoric,*[16] to some extent overlaps the scope of the present study.

There are also more general works that have helped to shape my own thinking, particularly the work of Milman Parry and Albert B. Lord on the patterns of epic oral singing among the bards of Yugoslavia.[17] It is plain that the role played in Yugoslav culture by the epic song is by no means identical with the role played in Israelite culture by prophetic words from Yahweh, and that these types of utterance contrast notably in the *degree of fixation* of their wording; nevertheless, the studies of Parry and Lord help the person who is oriented to the printed word to understand better how utterances of consequence function in an oral culture.

A justification is in order here for confining my attention in this study to the first twenty chapters of Jeremiah, for my case would surely have been strengthened by thorough attention to the total book of

Jeremiah. But in defense of the more limited approach offered here, I may say that it has been clear to me for some years, ever since Lundbom pointed out to me the "great inclusio" between the call-narrative in 1:4-10 and the final "confession" in 20:14-18, that chapters 1-20 embody the shape of an important early stage in the collection of material; Lundbom calls these chapters "an early major composition."[18] Thus this collection would afford ample scope for the development of analytical techniques which, if proved valid, could then be applied to the balance of the book. It seemed appropriate, then, to offer such a work-in-progress at this time, concentrating on the first twenty chapters and adding some suggestive remarks in a postscript regarding the material after Jer. 20 (see below, chap. 9).

Let us turn, then, to a fresh examination of these twenty chapters, bringing to the enterprise a conviction that ancient man was not altogether careless and foolish, but on the contrary was most solicitous in the task of recording and transmitting such material as is contained in the first part of the book of Jeremiah, arranging it in ways appropriate to his largely oral culture.

b. Methodology

Having said this much, however, I must go on to admit that one cannot be at all sure *what to look for* when he embarks upon a search for shape or structure in the material of the portion of the book of Jeremiah under consideration: it is simply not possible, *a priori,* to specify in detail the kinds of signs to look for by which one may establish structure. The technique will have to emerge in the course of a rather experimental and thoroughly inductive examination of the material. The constant questions must be simply: what is going on here?—what is happening, from the point of view of rhetoric? What is the relation of a given oracle or larger unit to what has come before and to what comes after? To what is it organically related? Does it offer fresh themes, fresh wording, fresh material of every sort? Or is it material which, though making a fresh departure, nevertheless employs earlier wording or themes? Or is it, on the contrary, some kind of reprise of earlier material, forming an inclusio? Or is it in fact a sudden intrusion into the continuity of material around it? In short, I shall be using the techniques of rhetorical criticism, not on small units, but on large blocks of material.[19] Again, I must repeat: to say *rhetorical criticism* is not necessarily to specify very clearly what I shall be about, because, by definition, rhetorical criticism analyzes what is unique and distinctive about a given unit of material, and therefore a description of its rhetorical form must inevitably proceed inductively, on the basis of the specificities before us. So, most simply, I can say: we shall be looking for repetitions, parallels, and contrasts in words, phrases, syntax, and other structures, to see what they can teach us.

When I have had occasion to discuss this project with colleagues, or share some of my conclusions, several kinds of objections have been leveled. I should like to discuss these now, to take account of them at least, if not to answer them totally.

First, the question is raised why I have not made more use of form criticism. The answer must be, because it does not apply in most of the circumstances with which I am dealing. A prime example will be the two "integrating oracles," as I shall call them, which function in the initial stratum of material in chapters 11-20 (I discuss the whole matter in 7, b). These two oracles, which rhetorically serve identical functions at successive stages of the collecting process, are 16:1-9 and 20:14-18. Now, from a form-critical point of view these oracles are completely contrastive: 16:1-9 is a (supplementary) call from God to Jeremiah, parallel with the (primary) call in chapter 1, while 20:14-18 is the final and most bitter "confession" of Jeremiah to God—thus an "individual lament." Further, these oracles help to integrate early material that is largely identical with what critics have come to call the "confessions" of Jeremiah. But to my knowledge 16:1-9 has never been counted as part of a "confessional" collection. Yet, I repeat, these two passages serve an identical rhetorical function, sharing verbal and assonantal echoes with earlier material in precisely the same kind of way. I can only conclude that form-criticism presents questions that can lead us to envisage the *Sitz im Leben* out of which a given unit comes, but evidently cannot help us to understand the process by which the units were collected and built into larger structures.

But I hasten to add that in some cases form-criticism is thoroughly relevant. From time to time I shall be led to offer a fresh exegesis of a given passage in order to understand how it fits rhetorically into its context; or, conversely, occasionally my rhetorical analysis will suggest a fresh exegesis. Structure and content always interact. And when it comes to the exegesis of a given minimum unit, form-criticism is an appropriate technique. A prime example is my rhetorical analysis of the way 17:5-8 fits into its context in the early collecting process, and my exegesis of that passage, both of which indicate that the passage is a "confession," to be laid alongside of the remainder of the commonly recognized "confessions" (see 7, i).

To put it in more general terms, I would suggest that by the time the collecting process began, the *Gattung* of a given unit was less important than the simple perception that "here is a word from God, or a word to God, that must not be lost," so that appropriate means were devised for the retention of these units. It is the location of those means that is my goal.

By the same token, I must say that in this inquiry I have tried to ignore the traditional rubrics of literary or source criticism—the judgments on "early" and "late" passages in Jeremiah's career, on oracles that are "genuine" or "nongenuine" to Jeremiah. I have even tried ignoring the contrast between poetry and prose, though I am well aware that there is a difference, and that poetic material and prose material come out of different *Sitze;* but I wanted to test whether the structures that appear to exist took shape *after* the mingling of poetic and prose material into one corpus. (The answer, in most cases, is negative.)

The bypassing of questions of form-criticism and literary criticism leads to an impression of "flatness" in the way the material is dealt with here, which strikes some of my colleagues as odd, as if the material were "all from the same cloth." But, I repeat, I am not turning my back on the findings of these other disciplines; rather, I am trying to focus on the collection process, and I hope that the techniques offered here are appropriate to the problem at hand.

Finally, many who have been patient enough to work through the details of the analysis given here respond with the judgment that it is too subtle; that one cannot expect ancient man to have paid so much attention to key words, to the balance of phonemes, or whatever; that no ancient collector could have been conscious of anything so intricate. But surely it is evident that there can be a great gap between structure that is *sensed* by a poet or artist, or by one who enjoys a work of art, on the one hand, and the *systematic analysis* of the structure by a critic, on the other. The one may be altogether subconscious; the other must of necessity be thoroughly conscious. I discussed this matter glancingly some time ago in another connection, when I described my pleasure in a well-known couplet of the poet Alexander Pope, and then my subsequent (and comparatively labored) analysis of the structure of that couplet.[20] We know with what seeming effortlessness Mozart and Schubert seem to have produced some of their musical works; it is left then to the musicologist to work out the analyses of the works in question, all the details of which the composers could hardly have been conscious of.

But we are in an even more difficult position than the musicologist with something from Mozart or Schubert; we are more in the position of a textual analyst of, say, the year A.D. 4000 who has unearthed the score of a Schubert string quartet, but who lacks any very clear notion of what a violin looks like or sounds like, and who at least at the beginning of his studies lacks any very clear notion of what our musical notation involves. He is reduced, then, for the moment, to finding patterns on the page that "echo" each other, that balance, patterns that seem to develop from earlier ones. He may be ready to defend his pattern analysis even without the ability to reproduce the music in any way at all. This, I submit, is very much our situation with respect to the material in the book of Jeremiah. We have no tunes; we have no gestures. We have only indirect hints, even, in the dialogue of chapters 4-6, as to who is speaking a given line. And yet all of this, and more, was presumably available to the ancient preserver of oral tradition, and most of the patterns that emerge for us only in the course of the most painful analysis would have been subliminally plain to the early hearer. This unit "belongs" with that unit. Why? The early hearer might not be able to say with too much precision, but they were nevertheless associated in his mind. For us, the process of isolating the factors by which one unit is bound to another must be far more deliberate and analytical.

All this is less than an exact science, and in particular there are two kinds of uncertainties that we shall have to face: the first, that often we shall not be able to determine with utter certainty that two or more occurrences of a word (or phrase or whatever) is a significant rhetorical tag; the second, that while we may be able in certain instances to determine with certainty that a given repetition is rhetorically significant, we may still be unable with complete certainty to determine *what that significance is.* Let me illustrate.

In 5:17 the verb *'kl*, "eat," appears four times. I shall suggest in the course of this investigation that these occurrences in 5:17 answer or balance in some way the single occurrence of *'kl* in 2:3. (The way the two verses balance each other must be specified later.) Now *'kl* is obviously no rare verb, and it appears in three other passages between 2:3 and 5:17, namely, 2:7, 2:30, and 3:24. The occurrence in 3:24 may have rhetorical significance with respect to 2:3 and 5:17, but those in 2:7 and 2:30 would seem to be rather casual occurrences of the verb. Plainly, then, if one is to draw up a convincing argument, one must depend upon *many* bits of interlocking data—the occurrences of *'kl* in these instances are hardly enough—and one must accept the fact that some at least of the argumentation of this study, though suggestive, will be something less than airtight. Fortunately, a good many of the words and phrases that I shall identify as rhetorical tags are unique to the material, and a large proportion of the footnotes in this study will simply offer data on the rarity of the word or phrase under discussion.

By the same token, we may sometimes be sure that we have located a rhetorical tag, but be less than sure what conclusion is to be drawn from the data regarding the process by which the material came to take its present shape. Thus the phrase *'ārûr hā'îš 'ašer* appears in 11:3 and 20:15, and nowhere else; the synonymous phrase *'ārûr haggeber 'ašer* appears in 17:5, and nowhere else: and there are no other candidates for analogous phrases to lay alongside these. Now how are we to interpret these data? Is 17:5 in inclusio with 11:3, and 20:15 evidence of later expansion, or is 17:5 in inclusio with 20:15 and this block in inclusio with 11:3? Or is 17:5 irrelevant to an inclusio between 11:5 and 20:15? All these models are theoretically possible; I shall opt for the second, for reasons that will be delineated later. The point here is that we may sometimes be quite sure that we have located data of rhetorical significance but be less sure what conclusions to draw.

And it should be emphasized once more that to establish the existence of structure does not necessarily imply an identification of the agent responsible for the structure (*i.e.*, Jeremiah, Baruch, or an anonymous editor). One may suspect that the primary strata of the material may be attributed to Jeremiah or Baruch, and secondary insertions to a later editor, but that suspicion (with which I shall deal systematically at the end of the study, in 10, b) is an entirely separate matter from the establishment of the *existence* of structure, the task to which we now turn.

1

The Call (1:4-14)

CHAPTER 1 of Jeremiah, which contains the call of the prophet, can be subdivided into four sections: the editorial superscription (vv. 1-3), the call proper (vv. 4-10), two visions (vv. 11-14), and expansions, largely in prose (vv. 15-19). The editorial superscription is plainly added at a late stage of the tradition.

The call proper gives every evidence of being the initial unit of material at the very beginning of the process of collection. The evidence of the "great inclusio," 1:5 with 20:14-18, already alluded to, *would not necessarily* argue for the presence of the call from the beginning of the collection process, for one could easily imagine an early collection of oracles against Judah and Jerusalem (the core of chapters 2-6, say) to which the call and the confessions would be added as an enlargement.

No, the crucial bit of evidence is that the word *na'ar,* "youth" (vv. 6, 7), is picked up in 2:2 (*n*^{e}*'ûrayik,* "your [time of] youth"); and 2:2-3 has a central role to play in the structure of chapters 2-6, as we shall see. It would be hard to imagine any process by which the call of Jeremiah, with the centrality of the word *na'ar,* would have come into the tradition at a later stage, given the presence of *ne'ûrayik* in 2:2.[1]

There follow then the two visions, of the almond branch (vv. 11-12) and of the pot facing away from the north (vv. 13-14). These visions, with *rō'eh* in vv. 11 and 13 (and *lir'ôt* in v. 12) are linked to the call by the occurrence of *re'ēh* in v. 10 (and as *re'ēh* may be linked to *'al-tîrā'* in v. 8 by assonance: final *aleph* was no doubt pronounced in Jeremiah's day).

The second vision obviously anticipates what I shall be calling the "foe cycle" in Jer. 4-6 (note, at this point, *miṣṣāpôn* and *(hā)rā'â* in 1:14 and 4:6). But there is no obvious association between the material in the first vision and what I shall be calling the *harlotry cycle* in chapters 2-3. There is, however, a possibility that I should like to suggest; it seems farfetched now, but may not appear so in the light of analogous suggestions proposed later in this study. The possibility is this: the word *maqqēl,* "rod, staff" (1:11), is by no means common, and its use here might well call up, in the mind of both hearer and compiler, the only earlier occurrence of this word in the pre-Jeremianic prophetic literature, namely, Hos. 4:12, "[my people] inquire of a thing of wood, and their staff *(ûmaqlô)* gives them oracles." The wording in Hosea continues: "For a spirit of harlotry *(rûaḥ zenûnîm)* has led them astray," and the by-form *zenût,* "harlotry," occurs in the previous verse, 4:11. To repeat: *maqqel* occurs nowhere else in the pre-Jeremianic prophetic literature, nor in the psalms, where a similar phraseology might be sought for; and since *zenût* appears in Jer. 3:2, and forms of the verb *znh* in 2:20 and 3:1,[2] I suggest that the *maqqēl*-vision, 1:11-12, is associated with the harlotry cycle, chapters 2-3, because of the association of wording in Hos. 4:11-12, paralleling the association of the pot-vision (1:13-14) with the foe cycle (chapters 4-6).[3] This pattern would then be similar to the "adjunction by secondary association," which we shall meet later (see 4, k; 10, a).

The expansions, largely in prose (1:15-19), will also be discussed later, in chapter 8; it looks very much as if these were added at a later stage to serve as parallels to additions that were being made elsewhere in the corpus.

I suggest, then, that the earliest collection of Jeremiah's words contained the call proper, 1:4-10, linked to 2:2 by the word *na'ar,* plus the two visions (1:11-14), which seem to be associated with the first two cycles (chapters 2-3 and 4-6) respectively.

2
The Harlotry and Foe Cycles; the Seed-Oracle (2:2-3)

a. Introduction

IT is obvious to anyone reading the material in Jer. 2-6 that there is a sharp break at 4:5; in general, the material in Jer. 2-3 is concerned with the harlotry of the nation, while the material in 4:5ff depicts the coming of a foe from the north. (I shall argue later, in 4, a, that the break actually comes with 4:1, but what is evident at this point is that there *is* a division into two blocks of material.) Now two points need to be made at the outset: first, that the material of 2:2-3 turns out to foreshadow these two blocks; and second, that it is necessary to establish terminology for the units of material with which I am dealing. I shall take these matters up in reverse order.

b. Terminology of the Units of Material

As one reads through the material of either of these two blocks, one is not sure of the nature of the units with which he is dealing. The block on harlotry in chapters 2-3—can one isolate one long poem of several sections?—or a collection of related poems that were perhaps conceived in some way as a unity as the individual poems took shape?—or does one have a miscellany of poems (separate "oracles") on related themes? Indeed, can one be sure where the boundaries are between the subdivisions? This is a basic problem that commentators have tried to solve, only to come up with a variety of solutions. I shall here beg the question by using terminology that does not commit me to any view of the isolatedness or integratedness of the subdivisions. I shall call the block on harlotry the *harlotry cycle,* and the block on the foe from the north the *foe cycle.* (I shall later locate a second foe cycle in chapters 8-10; this I shall call the *supplementary foe cycle.*) The basic subdivisions within each cycle I shall simply call *sections.* But because the unit 2:2-3 seems to function independently of both the harlotry and foe cycles, I shall call these two verses the *seed oracle.*

c. The Seed Oracle (2:2-3)

Chapter 2 begins with an oracle, vv. 2-3, that sets forth the pristine loyalty and purity of Israel. We have already seen that the word *n*e*'ûrayik* in this oracle (2:2) is linked to the key word *na'ar* in the call (1:6, 7). These two verses, as I have already intimated, turn out to foreshadow the material in both the harlotry and foe cycles; indeed, this foreshadowing is done quite systematically: 2:2 foreshadows the harlotry cycle, and 2:3 the foe cycle. How this is done we must now learn in detail.

The links between 2:2 and the harlotry cycle are clear: the words of 2:2 are matched systematically, in a kind of chiastic fashion, with what turn out to be the two halves of the harlotry cycle (2:5-37; 3:1-5, 12b-14a, 19-25) so as to map out the outlines of each half:

2:2	I (=Yahweh) remember			
		your (=Israel's) youth		
			bride	
				your following me (*hlk* qal) in the wilderness in a land not. . .
2:5				you went after worthlessness (*hlk* qal);
2:6				he who leads us (*hlk* hiphil) in the wilderness in a land not. . . and not. . .
2:32	forget forget me (=Yahweh)		bride	
3:4		my (=Israel's) youth		
3:21	forget Yahweh			
3:24		our (=Israel's) youth.		

That is to say, 2:5 and 2:32 are at the beginning and toward the end respectively of the first half of the harlotry cycle, and 3:4 and 3:21, 24 are toward the beginning and toward the end of the second half. These rhetorical tags appear nowhere else in the vicinity.

When I come to consider the structure of the foe cycle, I shall consider the parallel list of rhetorical tags in 2:3 that point toward that cycle (*i.e.*, "to Yahweh," the theme of harvest, "eat," and "evil came upon them".)[1] For now, I must document my findings regarding 2:2 and the harlotry cycle in more detail.

The link between the call (1:4-10) and the material in chapters 2ff is, as we have seen, *na'ar* (1:6, 7) and *n*[e']*ûrayik* (2:2). But *n*[e']*ûrayik* at the same time participates in the structure of what follows, as well as its parallel *k*[e]*lûlōtayik* and the accompanying verb *zkr*. In 2:2 Yahweh remembers the devotion of Israel; in 3:32 we are told that even though a bride never *forgets* her wedding garb, "my people have forgotten me days without number," and in 3:21 that "they have forgotten Yahweh their God."[2]

The word *n*[e']*ûrîm* appears otherwise in Jeremiah in 3:4 and 3:24,[3] so that the word forms an inclusio for the material in chapter 3.[4] The word *k*[e]*lûlôt* is not otherwise found in Jeremiah, but the noun *kallâ* is found in 2:32 with *škḥ*, "forget," as we have seen. (Question: Do we have a chiasmus here in the patterning of the nouns: concrete, abstract, abstract, concrete—*na'ar* 1:6, 7; *n*[e']*ûrayik* 2:2; *k*[e]*lûlōtayik* 2:2; *kallâ* 2:32? It is an appealing possibility.) We should also take note of the fact that the word *kallâ* also appears in a later poetic passage, at the end of 16:1-9, where it seems to serve in a later inclusio (see 7, b).[5]

To sum up so far: the words related to *bride* form an

inclusio in Jer. 2, and the words for *youth* form an inclusio in Jer. 3.

The three subsequent phrases in 2:2 help to generate the first section of chapter 2 (namely, vv. 5-13), as the chart has indicated. Thus *hlk* (qal) *'aḥ*^{a}*rê*, 2:2, is picked up in v. 5 "and they walked after worthlessness" and in v. 8 (as well as in vv. 23 and 25); and the verb in the form of a hiphil participle occurs in 2:6, followed by parallels to the other two phrases—"in the wilderness" (2:2) occurs again in 2:6, and "in a land not sown," 2:2, is mimicked by both "in a land none passes through" and "where no man dwells" (*b*^{e}*'ereṣ* followed by *lō'* and a defining word).[6]

3

The Harlotry Cycle (2:5-37, 3:1-5, 12b-14a, 19-25)

a. The First Half (2:5-37)

As we have already seen, the harlotry cycle breaks into two parts (the "bride" section and the "youth" section), the dividing line being the division between chapters 2 and 3; but when we turn to 2:5-37 to see how this material is organized and what its sections are, we are confronted by a problem of great difficulty. One senses directly that the material from verse 5 onward is divided into several sections, and that words, phrases, and themes taken up early in the passage turn up later in new forms—but it is not at all easy to reach any firm conclusions regarding the structure of the passage.

The first thing to notice is that the second-person references to Israel in chapter 2 vary in gender and number in what seems to be a patterned way. This does not seem to be the case in chapter 3; there, because of the way the imagery of "wife" and "sons" is treated, the second-person variations do not seem to be patterned; but in chapter 2 the boundaries at which the references change seem identical with the divisions within the chapter, which we sense from content and theme. The shifts are as follows:

[2:2	fem. sing.]
2:5-10	masc. pl.
2:16-25	fem. sing.
2:28	masc. sing.
2:29-30 (+31?)	masc. pl.
2:33-37	fem. sing.

(The uncertainly about v. 31 arises from the fact that the initial phrase of that verse, *haddōr 'attem rᵉ'û dᵉbar-yhwh*, ordinarily stricken from the poem by commentators as a gloss, may well mask material originally present and part of the poem, as I hope to show on another occasion.) Now the shift from masc. sing. to masc. pl. between vv. 28 and 29 might not prove too significant, but the shifts between masc. and fem. in this chapter certainly mark the boundaries of the units.

The first section is relatively easy to discern: it is vv. 5-13—a description of Israel's present situation (vv. 5-8) followed by the indictment of Israel by Yahweh (vv. 9-13). These two subsections form a unity; the second is consequent upon the first (*lākēn*, v. 9). Now, material from 2:2, as we have seen, helps to generate the material in the first half (vv. 5-8) of the first section;[1] and material in the first section forms assonantal links with the second half (vv. 9-13): thus *wayyēlᵉkû 'aḥᵃrê hahebel* (v. 5) and *wᵉ'aḥᵃrê lō-yô'ilû hālākû* (v. 8) help to generate *'ᵃšer lō'-yākilû hammāyim* (v. 13). It is clear, furthermore, that key words in vv. 5-13 help to generate the material in vv. 14-37.

Verse 14 begins a fresh section that seems to end with v. 19 (vv. 16ff offer fem. sing. references). The section is divided into two subsections (vv. 14-16, 17-19). These two subsections are united by the parallel initial interrogative *hª-* (vv. 14, 17). There is also a hint of parallelism of reference to nations in vv. 15-16 and v. 18: if "lions" in v. 15 is a reference to Assyria, as it is in Isa. 5:29,[2] then we have the chiastic structure "lions" = Assyria v. 15, Egypt v. 16; Egypt v. 18a, Assyria v. 18b.

Though the material in vv. 14-16 moves off in a new direction in comparison with that of vv. 5-13, nevertheless there are words and phrases here that do seem to echo 2:3 (in the seed oracle) and 2:6 (at the beginning of the first section of the harlotry cycle). Verse 14 begins with the phrase *hª'ebed yiśrā'ēl*, in contrastive parallelism with the earlier nominal clause *qōdeš yiśrā'ēl* in 2:3. In v. 15 there is a reminiscence of v. 6: *mibbᵉli yōšēb,* v. 15, echoes *wᵉlō'-yāšab 'ādām šām* in v. 6. Then in v. 16, the striking word *qodqōd* might well be a reminder of *qōdeš (yiśrā'ēl)* in 2:3. And in vv. 17-19 we have a solid texture of reminiscences of vv. 5-13: in v. 17 the verbs *'śh* and *'zb,* echoing their occurrence in v. 13, and the participle *môlîk*, echoing its previous occurrence in v. 6.[3] Finally, the construct *mê* in v. 18 echoes *hammāyim* in v. 13.

Though the second-person references remain fem. sing. in vv. 20-25, there is fresh material here that speaks not of the political situation with Egypt and Assyria, but of Israel's conduct with the Baals. And again vv. 20-25 are divided into two subsections with strong unity within each half.

Verses 20-23: four images triggered by earlier prophetic material—

(1) v. 20a—the intractable animal (cf. Isa. 1:2, Hos. 10:11)
(2) v. 20b—the harlot (cf. Hos. 4:13)
(3) v. 21—the vine gone wild (cf. Isa. 5:2, Hos. 10:1)
(4) v.22—one guilty of bloodshed (cf. Isa. 1:15)

Verses 23-25:
v. 23a—introduction, with "say," "go after," followed by two imperatives;
  v. 23b—image of the young camel
  v. 24—image of the wild ass
v. 25—conclusion, with two imperatives, followed by "say" and "go after."

But the two subsections are united as well:
v. 20: *wattō'm^eri lō'*
v. 23: *'êk tō'm^erî lō'*. . .
v. 21: *'êk*

And just as vv. 14-19 echo both 2:3 on the one hand and 2:6 and 13 on the other, so vv. 20-25 echo both vv. 14-19 and v. 7. Specifically, one finds the verb *'bd* in v. 20 echoing *'ebed* in v. 14, and *r^e'i. . .d^e'î* in v. 23 echoing *ûd^e'û ûr^e'û* in v. 19 (with reversal of order of the verbs). On the other hand, the verb *ṭm'* in v. 23 echoes the occurrence of the verb in v. 7.[4]

It may be noted in passing the v. 20 may offer a very nice assonance to v. 2. In a study of the hierarchy of occurrences of the phrase "on every high hill and under every green tree" that I made some years ago,[5] I suggested that the phrase is based originally on Hos. 4:13, as subsequently summarized by Deut. 12:2; obviously the phrase was widely imitated, both within the book of Jeremiah (3:6, 13; 17:2) and outside it. Now, one notes, in examining v. 20, the nice assonances of the verse: *g-b-ā* plus *g-b-ā* in the first colon, *'s* plus *s'* in the second and third. But I would go on to suggest that the word *ra'ᵃnān* and the double occurrence of *kol-* here reflect the *na'ar* plus *kallā* combination that is set forth in v. 2. The word *kol-* was pronounced *kull-* in Jeremiah's day, and it is to be noted that v. 20 contains the first occurrences of *kol-* since v. 2; and further, neither furtive *pataḥ* nor disyllabic segholates existed for Jeremiah, so that we would have:

na'r̲	v. 20: *ra'nān*
kallā	v. 20: *kull-*.

Permutation of consonants certainly plays a role in the structural devices of Jer. 1-20 (for a particularly remarkable example, see below, 7, b), and it is altogether likely that in this opening verse of the section there should be an echo of the key words in v. 2 with which we have been dealing.

Verses 26ff begin a fresh unit. The second-person reference changes from fem. sing. in v. 25 to masc. sing. in v. 28, and the "thief" reference in v. 26 is not parallel to images such as that of "harlot" in vv. 20-25: those in vv. 20-25 were metaphors, while v. 26 offers a simile (*kᵉ*, "like").[6]

One does not need to demonstrate in detail that the remainder of the chapter consists of three units: vv. 26-28, 29-32, 33-37; all the commentaries sense a break between vv. 28 and 29, and between vv. 32 and 33, and the shifts of second-person references indicate that this analysis is sound. The question is, how are these units related to each other and to what has come before?

One might imagine that they form three subsections in an A-B-A' pattern with respect to each other. It is true, there are certainly strong thematic and verbal unities between vv. 26-28 and vv. 33-37: the verb *mṣ'* in v. 26 once, in v. 34 twice; the verb *bwṣ̌* in v. 26 twice, in v. 36 twice. In addition, one finds "thief" in v. 26 and "breaking in" in v. 34.

But the notion that the three subsections here form an A-B-A' pattern is false; the basic form is A-A'-B. The middle subsection, vv. 29-32, forms a very strong balance to vv. 26-28, and both subsections together serve as a kind of inclusio back to the beginning of chapter 2; the last subsection, vv. 33-37, offers no particular balance with the beginning of chapter 2, but instead picks up characteristics of later sections (vv. 14-19, vv. 20-25) and of the first subsection (vv. 26-28—hence the illusion of an A-B-A' pattern!) to form a transition to the material in chapter 3. I shall now substantiate this analysis.

The two subsections, vv. 26-28 and vv. 29-32, are parallel, but the parallelism is subtly contrived. Each section contains a simile: *k*^{e}*bōšet gannāb*, "like the shame of a thief," v. 26, and *k*$^{e'}$*aryeh mašḥît*, "like a destroying lion," v. 30. There are no other occurrences of the preposition *k*^{e}- in chapter 2 outside of these vv. 26-32; one more occurrence of *k*^{e}- will be reconstructed from the LXX of v. 28 in a moment.

The next parallel to notice is the use of *mispār*, "number": it appears at the head of the last colon of v. 28 in the MT and at the end of the last colon of v. 32. But the last colon of v. 28 in the MT needs a balancing colon, which the LXX has preserved; Ewald saw this a century ago,[7] and he has been followed by Cornill, Volz,

Condamin, and Rudolph.[8] My own reconstruction differs slightly from those of the other commentators: the LXX begins with *kai kat' arithmon,* "and according to the number," which suggests that the first word of the Hebrew line is *ûk^emispar*, not *ûmispar* as they have it. The Hebrew line would then read: *ûk^emispar husôt y^erûšalaim qitt^erû labba'al*. This brings a third occurrence of *k^e*-, and a third occurrence of *mispar,* and brings, too, a nice chiasmus of *k^e*- and *kî*:

v. 26: *k^e*-. . .*kî*. . .
v. 28: *ki mispar*. . .
k^emispar. . .

Now in 3:24 the word *bōšet* "shame" is used as a euphemism for Baal (see below, 3, b). Here in chapter 2 we have v. 28 ending with *labba'al* (in the text restored from the LXX) and v. 26 beginning with *k^ebōšet; bōšet*, note well, is not *in this passage* a euphemism for Baal, but it does function in this way elsewhere, and it looks as if this double meaning serves to create an inclusio for vv. 26-28. Now v. 30 begins with *laššāw'*, "in vain," and the word *šāw'* functions in 18:15 as a euphemism for Baal. It appears then that v. 26 and v. 30 each begin with nouns that serve *elsewhere* in Jeremianic poetry as euphemisms for Baal. That this seeming parallelism by secondary function elsewhere is not an illusion is shown by the wording of 18:15:

kî š^ekēḥûnî 'ammî	"for my people have forgotten me,
laššāw' y^eqaṭṭērû	to Vanity they burn incense."

We see that *'ammî š^ekēḥûnî*, "my people have forgotten me" (with word order reversed), occurs in the last line of 2:32; *laššāw'*, "in vain/to Vanity," occurs at the beginning of v. 30, and *y^e^qaṭṭ^e^rû* is the imperfect of the same verb whose perfect was restored from the LXX in the last colon of v. 28. In short, a line of poetry genuine to Jeremiah occurs elsewhere that combines the diction of 2:26-28 and 2:29-32. The parallelism between *k^e^bōšet* and *laššāw'*, in that both serve elsewhere as euphemisms of Baal, is genuine.

One might go on then to suggest that the preposition *l^e^-* plus definite article in *laššāw'*, v. 30, is balanced by the double *l^e^-* plus definite article in *lā'ēṣ w^e^lā'eben* in v. 27 (and by the presumed *labba'al* in v. 28). The overall patterning that then emerges is as follows:

v. 26: *k^e^bōšet gannāb kî*. . .
v. 27: . . .*lā'ēṣ*
. . .*w^e^lā'eben*
v. 28: *kî mispar*. . .
ûk^e^mispar. . .*labba'al*
v. 30: *laššāw'*. . .
. . .*k^e^'aryēh*
v. 32: . . .*mispār*.

When the material is laid out in this fashion, the structure of vv. 30-32 is seen to be a compressed reflection of that of vv. 26-28. Verse 29 stands outside this structure; it serves the function of beginning the reminiscence back to the beginning of chapter 2 (*tārîbû 'ēlāy* here reflects *'ārîb 'itt^e^kem* in v. 9) which is so strongly completed by "bride" and "forget" in v. 32, words which of course reflect v. 2. One may go on to say that there may be other features of the material in vv. 26-32 that both reflect its inner structure and exhibit its relationship to what has come before in the chapter: thus there may be a balance between "my father" (v. 27) and "your sons" (v. 30) which reflects "your fathers" (v. 5) and (your sons) (v. 9).

By this reading of the evidence, vv. 33-37 serve to balance in summary fashion the material in chapter 2 from verse 14 onward. For if vv. 30-32 compress the framework found in vv. 26-28, vv. 33-37 expand the framework found in vv. 14-19. This is clear from the following parallel:

v. 14: *h*^{a}-, *'im-*, *maddû*^{a}‘	v. 31: *h*^{a}-, *'im-*, *maddû*^{a}‘
v. 17: *h*^{a}-	v. 32: *h*^{a}-
v. 18a: *mâ*. . .*l*^{e}- (+ infin.)	v. 33a: *mâ*. . .*l*^{e}- (+ infin.)
	v. 33b: *gam-*. . .
	v. 34: *gam-*. . .
v. 18b: *mâ*. . .*l*^{e}- (+ infin.)	v. 36a: *mâ*. . .*l*^{e}- (+ infin.)
	v. 36b: *gam-*. . .
	v. 37: *gam-*. . .

That is to say, the poet has taken the pattern of vv. 31-32, which is identical with that in vv. 14, 17, and has then built up an expanded framework for vv. 33-37 on the basis of v. 18.

Verse 35 does not enter into this scheme (as v. 29 did not enter into the scheme of the patterning of vv. 26-32?), but it is v. 35 which in wording reflects the material in vv. 20-25: *wattō'm*^{e}*rî*, "and you said," and *'al-'ōmrēk lō, ḥāṭā'tî*, "for saying, I have not sinned" (v. 35), reflect *'ēk tō'm*^{e}*ri lō' niṭmē'ti*, "how can you say, I am not defiled" (v. 23) and *wattō'm*^{e}*ri nô'āš lō'*, "and you said, it is hopeless, no" (v. 25). In addition, the phrase "I bring you to judgment" in v. 35 reflects the substantive concern of v. 29, where the verb *ryb* has judicial overtones.

Finally, of course, vv. 33-37 reflect the word usage in vv. 26-28 which we have already noticed: *mṣ'* "find," vv. 26, 34, and *bwš* "shame," vv. 26, 36. In short, vv. 26-37 manage to reflect quite systematically all of the preceding material in chapter 2: vv. 29-32 reflect the seed oracle and the first section, vv. 2-13, and vv. 33-37 reflect the second and third sections as well as the beginning of the fourth (vv. 26-28). I have had occasion elsewhere to analyze instances in which the conclusion of a poem reflects in a summarizing sort of way everything that has preceded it,[9] so that this kind of structure is not unexpected.

Verses 26-37, and especially vv. 33-37, point forward toward chapter 3 as well. If the word *bwš* helps to hold vv. 26-28 to vv. 33-37, then the permutation of that verb, *šwb* qal "return," occurs in v. 35 and thus prepares the way for its multiple occurrences in chapter 3. And if one looks for other anticipations of chapter 3, he will find them: the linking of *midbār* and *'ereṣ* (v. 31) is both an echo of 2:6 and an anticipation of 3:2; and *'ābî* "my father" and *'attâ* "thou" (v. 27) occur again in 3:4.

If now one backs away from the details, can he see a grand plan to the structure of chapter 2? I believe so.

The climax of vv. 5-13 is the point at which Yahweh affirms that he is the fountain of living waters (v. 13); this affirmation is balanced in v. 31 by the rhetorical question posed by Yahweh: "Have I been a wilderness to Israel, or a land of thick darkness? Why then. . .?" This interrogative passage, with its structure of *hᵃ-*, *'im-*, *maddûaʿ*, is balanced by the similar rhetorical questions, with *hᵃ-*, *'im-*, *maddûaʿ*, regarding Israel in v. 14: "Is Israel a slave? Is he a home-born servant? Why then. . .?" That is to say, the fourth section echoes the first section in the matter of the identity of God, and echoes the second section in posing rhetorical questions. Once we see this, we recognize that all four sections, as well as the seed oracle, are about *identifications,* and we have the following scheme:

[2:3—Israel is the possession of Yahweh]

A. 2:5-13:
   2:13—I (Yahweh) am the fountain of living waters
B. 2:14-19:
   2:14—Is Israel a slave? or a home-born servant? Why then. . .?
C. 2:20-25:
   2:20-25—you (Israel) are: (by implication) an intractable animal,
   a harlot
   a vine gone wild
   (by implication) one guilty of bloodshed
   a young camel
   a wild ass
D. 2:26-37:
   2:32—Have I (Yahweh) become a wilderness to Israel? or a land of deep darkness? Why then. . .?

The seed oracle, then, sets forth the primal covenantal bond between Israel and Yahweh. The first section asks why the fathers should have gone off from this bond and affirms Yahweh as the fountain of living waters. The second section raises the political question, why Israel should be a slave to foreign nations; the third section spills a whole kaleidoscope of metaphorical false identities for Israel, and the fourth section asks rhetorically why Israel should treat Yahweh as the opposite of the fountain of living waters.

There is one more structural observation that must be made at this point. As we shall discover when we examine 8:4ff (4, o), that passage is divided into two subsections: 8:4-7, which is introduced by the threefold question-form *h*^{a}-, *'im-*, *maddû*^{a}ʿ (8:4), and 8:8-10a, 13, which is introduced by *'ēkâ tō'm*^{e}*rû* (8:8). That passage (8:4-10a, 13) will be called the "postlude" to the foe cycle when we come to examine the structure of that part of the book of Jeremiah, and as such will serve, not only as a part of an inclusio to close the foe cycle, but to round off the harlotry cycle as well. As the closing portion of an inclusio that helps to round off the harlotry cycle, we shall see that it offers a structure that mimics in abbreviated form the structure of the first half of the harlotry cycle (*i.e.,* 2:5-37), and thus helps us to clarify the structure of the material now under consideration. Once more one must set forth the material in parallel columns, using for the sections of chapter 2 the capital letters already employed:

B. 2:14-19:	
2:14—*h*^{a}-, *'im-*, *maddû*^{a}ʿ	8:4—*h*^{a}-, *'im-*, *maddû*^{a}ʿ
C. 2:20-25:	
2:20—*wattō'm*^{e}*rî*	
2:21—*w*^{e}*'ēk*	
2:23—*'ēk tō'm*^{e}*rî*	8:8—*'ēkâ tō'm*^{e}*rû*
D. 2:26-37:	
2:31—*h*^{a}-, *'im-*, *maddû*^{a}ʿ	
2:35—*wattō'm*^{e}*rî*	

b. The Second Half (3:1-5, 12b-14a, 19-25)

Though I have designated the material in this part of the harlotry cycle the "second half," and have designated verse numbers for the material in the title of this section of the study, neither the designation nor the extent of this section can be taken for granted. It is clear that there is much secondary material within chapter 3, and it is difficult to avoid circular reasoning as we attempt to locate the material here that participates in any basic structure, *and* to discern that structure. We must proceed with care.

The strong feeling of commentators today is that 3:19 follows directly onto 3:5, and that 4:1-4 forms a conclusion to the material in chapter 3.[10] I disagree with both judgments and will suggest instead that 4:1-4 belongs with the "foe cycle" of 4:5ff and that 3:12b-14a belongs where it is found, between 3:1-5 and 19-25, as indicated in the title of this section of the study. We must examine the evidence, and deal with the issues through three questions: (1) Is 4:1-4 to be included in this half of the harlotry cycle? (2) How much of the MT of 3:1-25 is to be included? (3) How does the material to be included divide itself into sections?

(1) Does 4:1-4 belong here? All the commentators affirm this;[11] the repetitions of various forms of the root *šwb* would seem to demand it. I shall present an analysis later (4, a) that 4:1-4 serves rather as a "prelude" to the foe cycle, and is in this way in balance with the "postlude," 8:4ff, so that we must forgo a discussion of this matter for the present.

(2) There is no question about vv. 1-5. And let us leave the MT as it is, rather than emending *hā'āreṣ* in v. 1 to *hā'iššâ* with the LXX: we not only have the same verb and noun in the *pesher* in v. 9, but the same verb and noun in 23:15.

There is no question about vv. 19-23, either. Further, there is a poetic core to vv. 24-25, as Rudolph has rightly pointed out, and I follow his reconstruction here.[12] The prose insertions in these verses are: "their flocks and their herds, their sons and their daughters," an insertion from 5:17, where the same verb, *'kl,* appears in a parallel context; and "we and our fathers from our youth even to this day" and "we have sinned against Yahweh our God." When these are removed, the result is:

v.24: *wᵉhabbōšet 'ākᵉlâ*
'et-yᵉgîaʿ 'ᵃbôtênû minnᵉʿûrênû
v. 25: *niskᵉbâ bᵉboštenû*
ûtᵉkassenû kᵉlimmatenû
kî lō' šamaʿnû
bᵉqôl yhwh 'ᵉlohênû.

Now vv. 6-18 obviously represent a mixture of material. The prose *pesher* in vv. 6-11 makes a specific contrast between Israel and Judah, using several phrases from the poetry in the vicinity: *mᵉšûbâ yiśra'ēl* from v. 12b, the "high hill," "green tree" and "harlot" from 2:20, *'ēlay tašûb* from 4:1, and, with slightly different wording, echoes of 3:1, the root *bgd* from 3:20 and so on. Similarly, the material in vv. 14b-18 represents one or more exilic or postexilic additions.[13] Verse 12a is an explanatory rubric that breaks into the flow of the poetry, whether or not it is a valid memory of the original application of the poem. The words *under every green tree* in v. 13 are surely extraneous, a phrase inserted from 2:20. And I would retain *dᵉrākayik* rather emending (with Cornill and Rudolph) to *dôdayik* in v. 13: the word *derek* participates in the symmetry of the material, as we shall see. I retain, then, vv. 12b-14a (except "under every green tree"). This short poem gives every evidence of being genuine to Jeremiah: there is the inclusio of the double use of *šwb* in vv. 12b and 14a, and the balance of *pšʿ* and *šmʿt(-)* in v. 13.

But even though original to Jeremiah, do vv. 12b-14a belong in this location, or do they belong elsewhere in this part of the harlotry cycle, or are they altogether secondary to any structure of the harlotry cycle?

It must be admitted that there is strong evidence for seeing vv. 6-18, prose overlay and poetic core alike, as intrusive upon vv. 5 + 19. (a) The verb *qr'* and the noun *'ābî* appear in both vv. 4 and 19, and the bringing of vv. 5 and 19 together would bring these parallels of phraseology side by side, where their ironic contrast becomes effective: in vv. 4-5 the people call Yahweh "my Father" while continuing to do wrong, while in vv. 19-20 Yahweh expresses the expectation he had had that the people would say "my Father" and do right. (b) The themes of the land polluted (v. 2) and of the pleasant land, God's heritage (v. 19), would be brought closer together; they are side by side in 2:7 (and in reverse order there!), and this echo in chapter 3 is surely intentional.

On the other hand, in a structure of the form A-B-A'-B' the elements A and A' may have much in common, may demand to be heard as parallel, and yet be separated by B if B can be shown to anticipate B'. I submit that such is the case here—vv. 12b-14a function as element B, separating vv. 1-5 (A) and vv. 19ff (A') from each other. Further, there is some indication that vv. 12b-14a have their own echoes of vv. 1-5, which must be acknowledged. (a) The last line of v. 12 answers the question of v. 5: "Will he be angry forever?" with "I will not be angry forever." Admittedly vv. 12b-14a might have been inserted secondarily precisely in order to answer that question, but at least we can say that the passage fits where it stands. (b) Though the imperative *ûr*^{e}*'î* in v. 2 would seem to be in close balance to *ś*^{e}*'î* in the same verse, nevertheless the companion to *r*^{e}*'î* in both 2:19 and 2:23, namely, *d*^{e}*'î*, appears in v. 13, and can be understood as balancing *r*^{e}*'î* in some sense. (c)

There is a quite lovely chiasmus in the assonances with *šwb* in vv. 12b plus 14a and v. 22:

v. 12b: *šûbâ m^e^šûbâ yiśrā'ēl* v. 22: *šûbû bānîm šôbābîm*

v. 14a: *šûbû bānîm šôbābîm* *'erpâ m^e^šûbōtêkem*

(d) Indeed, we can now see a symmetry to the references to "father" and "sons" in the chapter:

v. 4—"my Father"
v. 14a—"sons"
v. 19—"my Father"
vv. 21, 22—"sons" (twice)
v. 24—"our fathers"

There are two other bits of symmetry between vv. 12b-14a and vv. 21ff that are more subtle, but still play a part, I suspect. (e) There were scattered references to Baal in chapter 2—2:8 *babba'al*; 2:23, *habb^e^'ālîm*; 2:28 LXX, *labba'al*. In chapter 3 we have two deformed references to Baal: in v. 14a, *ki 'ānōki bā'altî bākem*—in periphrastic translation, "for I was the one who functioned as your [true] Baal"; and in v. 24, *w^e^habbōšet 'āk^e^lâ*—"and the Shame has devoured," where the standard euphemism for Baal is evidently used deliberately because of the parallel with "let us lie down in our shame" in v. 25. (f) If one lists the occurrences of *derek* in chapters 2 and 3 and notes the syntax and nuances of meaning, one finds symmetry:

chapter 2	chapter 3
2:17—*badderek*—prep.; "path"	
2:18—*ladderek*—prep.; "path"	3:2—*'al-d^e^rākîm*—prep.; "path"
2:18—*ladderek*—prep.; "path"	
2:23—*darkēk*—accus.; "path"? "habit"?	
—*d^e^rākêha*—accus.; "tracks"	

2:33—*'et-d^erākayik*—accus.; "taught your ways" = "habits"	3:13—*'et-d^erākayik*—accus.; "scatter your ways" = "habits"
2:36—*'et-darkek*—accus.; "change your ways"	3:21—*'et-darkām*—accus.; "pervert their way".

This is to say, chapter 3 offers three occurrences of *derek:* the first is a plural with preposition in a concrete meaning that roughly parallels three occurrences of the singular with preposition in a concrete meaning in 2:17-18; and the second and third are with possessive suffixes, both with *'et- (nota accus.),* and these parallel the occurrences in 2:33 and 36 respectively: the first of each pair is a plural, the second of each pair is a singular, and the verbs correspond closely in meaning also. This sequence seems striking enough to reinforce my conviction that 3:13 (and thus 3:12b-14a) belongs where it is now located.

Let us now take a closer look at "my Father" in 3:4. There is little doubt in my mind that *'ābî* "my father" in 3:4 implies "my husband." This has been doubted: Duhm, Giesebrecht, and Rudolph all excise the word here as spoiling the wife motif, but Volz and the Koehler-Baumgartner Lexicon defend the nuance *husband* and so the integrity of the text.[14] The meaning "my husband" in 3:4 would make a nice balance to *k^elûlōtāyik*, "your bridehood," in 2:2. (For an analogous pattern in 12:6 + 15:10, see the discussion in 7, d.)[15] Furthermore, now that I may have established the meaning of "my husband" for *'ābî*, we can see how the phrase *ki 'ānōkî ba'altî* in v. 14a would offer ironic contrast!

(3) We are now ready to work out a division of chapter 3 into sections: I have already anticipated my answer in the remarks above on the structural pattern A-B-A'-B', and in the alternation of references to "father" and "sons." The sections will be: vv. 1-5,

12b-14a, 19-20, and 21-25. Some other details will reinforce this analysis.

(a) There is no way to divide vv. 1-5 any further. When we examine the passage, we see an inclusio of *hēn,* "behold" (v. 1), and *hinnēh,* "behold" (v. 5),[16] enclosing a double occurrence of *h*ᵃ- in v. 1 and again in vv. 4-5; and between the two pairs of questions, we find three occurrences of the root *znh,* in vv. 1, 2, and 3. These words may not be the only means to elucidate the structure of this section, but I see nothing more significant that would argue for a structure other than a simple A-B-A' for these verses.

(b) Again, in vv. 12b-14a there would seem to be a similar A-B-A' form: we note the second-person masc. sing. and pl. references with *šwb* in v. 12b, the fem. sing. in v. 13, and the masc. pl. again with *šwb* in v. 14a. This mixture of references, which occurs because of the blending of the images of "wife" and "sons," is in contrast to the situation in 2:5-37, in which the second-person references are distinct in gender and number.

(c) Verses 19-20 reflect vv. 1-5 in ways already described: the parallel of polluted land and pleasant land, the use of *qr'* and *'ābî,* and the reference to the faithless wife. This section is too short to have any elaborate structure of its own.

(d) Verses 21ff make up the fourth section; is it the last? At first glance one might think of a fourth section (vv. 21-23) and a coda (vv. 24-25): one sees *'ākēn* rounding off v. 20, and the parallel double use of *'ākēn* in v. 23. But it would seem best, after all, to keep the analysis simple—we note the inclusio of *qôl* plus *šm'* in the first phrase of v. 21 and the last phrase of v. 25.

This fourth section not only echoes the third *('ākēn),* but (since the third echoes the first) the second as well—the multiple use of *šwb,* and the euphemism for Baal: these symmetries have already been discussed.

A final section also typically echoes material from the beginning, and so we have the inclusio of *nᵉʿûrênû* (v. 24) with *nᵉʿûray* (v. 4), which has already been discussed, an inclusio that links chapter 3 to the seed oracle; and one more link with the seed-oracle—*'kl* in v. 24, which mimics 2:3 (and 2:30)—when Israel was faithful to Yahweh, foreign nations who tried to devour Israel were punished, but when Israel turned her devotion instead to Baal and sought food from him, ironically he devoured the substance built up by Israel over many generations.

There is one more link between this fourth section and the first section of chapter 3: *šᵉp̄ayim* (v. 21) echoes the occurrence of the word in v. 2.[17]

There are also, of course, a variety of links between the two halves of the harlotry cycle (chapters 2 and 3). The poet begins the cycle by addressing the nation about "your fathers" (2:5), and the cycle ends as the nation acknowledges what has been done by "our fathers" (3:25): this is a more substantial balance (plural possessive, reference to *ancestors*) that the one with "my Father" in the first and third sections of chapter 3 (singular possessive, reference to God).

Finally, I should like to revert to a link that I suggested in the discussion of 2:26-37, by which that passage is bound to chapter 3: that is that matter of the verbs *bwš* and *šwb.* We recall that two occurrences of *bwš* in 2:26 and two in 2:36 enclose a single occurrence of *šwb* qal in 2:35.[18] We are prepared, then, for the array of occurrences of *šwb* qal and the related noun *mᵉšûbâ* and adjective *šôb̄ab*) in chapter 3. Chapter 3 is then rounded off by two more occurrences of *bwš* at the end—*habbōšet* in v. 24 and *b*ᵉ*bošt*ē*nû* in v. 25. One may note that the association of *šwb* with *bwš* is not fortuitous: there is a nice assonance between *šābû* and *bōšû* in 14:2 and 14:(3?) 4 respectively.

It is pleasing to see the material of chapter 3 falling into four sections just as the material of 2:5-37 did, and to see a general parallel between the second and fourth sections of chapter 3 (the patterning of *šwb,* the displaced references to Baal), which might be analogous to the general parallel between the second and fourth sections of chapter 2 (*h*ᵃ-, *'im, maddûa*ʿ, plus an additional *h*ᵃ-). And we may raise the question whether there is not a nice echo of the third section of chapter 2 in the third section of chapter 3:

2:23—*'ēk tō'm*ᵉ*rî*
3:19—*w*ᵉ*'ānōkî 'amartî 'ēk.*[19]

One more point: we have had short one- or two-word quotations all along in the harlotry cycle (2:6, 8, 20, etc.), and in 3:22b-25 we have a long speech of the people that seems to indicate genuine repentance; this "dialogue" material prepares the way for the material in the foe cycle, where dialogue is constant.

My conclusion: the material of the harlotry cycle is far too richly textured to be amenable to easy precision in structural analysis, but I submit that the analysis given here is close to the original intent of the compiler.

4

The Foe Cycle (4:1-6:30; 8:4-10a, 13)

a. The Prelude (4:1-4) and Postlude (8:4-10a, 13)

THERE is a marked change of style at 4:5; from this point onward we hear the sounds of battle and meet the foe from the north. The first four verses of chapter 4, with their use of *swb,* seem to continue the material of chapter 3, so that (as we have seen)[1] commentators unanimously take 4:1-4 to be the closing section of the material that begins in 3:1.

Several pieces of evidence, however, combine to indicate that 4:1-4 is one-half of an "envelope" around the material on the foe from the north, 8:4-10a, 13 being the other half: what I have chosen here to call the *prelude* and *postlude* to the foe cycle.

(a) The inclusio of *nᵉʿûrîm* in 3:4 and 24 suggests that 3:25 rounds off that material.

(b) The closest analogue for the double use of verbal forms of *šwb* in 4:1 (*'im-tāšûb yiśrā'ēl. . . .'ēlay tāšûb)* is not in chapter 3 but in 8:4: *'im-yāšûb w^{e}lō' yāšûb*, a parallel that then suggests an inclusio around the total foe cycle.[2]

(c) Both 4:1-2 and 8:4-5 echo material within the foe cycle proper, *and adjoining verses respectively of that material*. Specifically, following the double occurrence of *šwb* in 4:1, we have, in v. 2: *w^{e}nišba'tā ḥay-yhwh be'^{e}met*, "and (if) you swear "as Yahweh lives" in truth," a parallel to *w^{e}'im ḥay-yhwh yō'merû, lākēn laššeqer yiššābē'û*, "and if they say 'as Yahweh lives,' then they swear falsely," in 5:2.[3] And following the double occurrence of *šwb* in 8:4, we have, in v. 5: *heḥ^{e}zîqû battarmît mē'^{a}nû lāšûb*, a parallel to *ḥizz^{e}qû p^{e}nêhem missela' mē^{a}nû lāšûb* in 5:3. This is the only occurrence of *šwb* in the foe cycle proper (4:5-6:30).[4] That is to say, 4:1-2 and 8:4-5 not only point to each other, but both point toward 5:2-3.

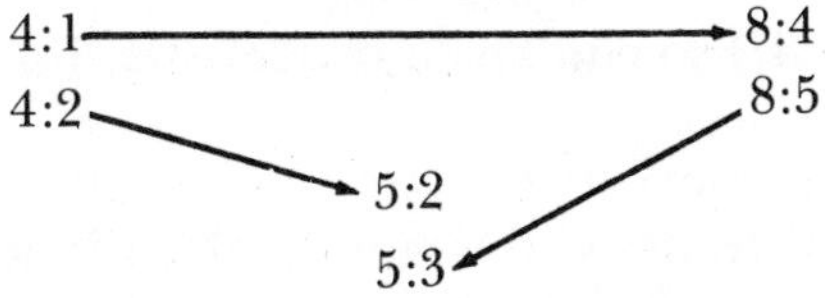

We must conclude that 4:1-4 and 8:4ff have used the double occurrence of *šwb* to form an "envelope" around the foe cycle, and in so doing have made a link between the foe cycle and the *šwb* material in the harlotry cycle in chapter 3.

Verses 3-4 echo two bits of pre-Jeremianic material, as the commentators point out: "break up your fallow ground" is modeled on Hos. 10:12, and "circumcise yourselves to Yahweh, remove the foreskin of your hearts" is an echo of Deuteronomy (10:16, 30:6). There is both unity and disunity between vv. 1-2 and 3-4.

There is unity, in that v. 2b also is a reminiscence of pre-Jeremianic material (the promises of God to Abraham in Genesis, most closely in Gen. 22:18), and in that *hasirû* in v. 4 and *tasîr* in v. 1 form an inclusio. On the other hand, there is disunity as well between vv. 1-2 and 3-4: the second-person-singular forms in vv. 1-2 give way to plural forms in vv. 3-4, so that both Giesebrecht and Weiser separate the two sections from each other.

As I shall suggest when I discuss 10:23-25, the quotations here in the prelude evidently function in an inclusio with those verses in chapter 10. There is a possibility, then, though I make it only as a hesitant suggestion, that 4:1-2 was the original form of the prelude, and that vv. 3-4 were added here when the "supplementary foe cycle," of which 10:23-25 forms the conclusion, was added to the growing corpus of Jeremiah material.[5]

We have already noted the parallel between 4:2 and 5:2, outside the prelude, and may now note further that *lᵉyhwh* in 4:4 echoes *lᵉyhwh* in 2:3 and anticipates *lᵉyhwh* in 5:10.[6]

A detailed analysis of the "postlude," 8:4-10a, 13, is best postponed until 4,o.

b. The Foe Cycle Proper (4:5-6:30): Echoes of the Seed Oracle (2:2-3)

Let us now return to a matter left undetailed above (2,c): there it was stated that a phrase in the opening seed oracle, *ra'â tabô' 'ᵃlêhem*, "evil came upon them" (2:3), helps to generate material in the foe cycle. I must now offer the data for this assertion.

This phrase occurs often in Jeremiah, but in so many variations that the problem becomes how to define the pattern. (a) Defined as *ra'â* plus a qal form of *bw'* plus *'al* and a suffix, the phrase occurs (beyond 2:3) in 5:12[7] and, outside the book of Jeremiah, significantly in Mic. 3:11 (the significance of this datum will be discussed in a moment). (b) With a hiphil participle ("I am bringing evil upon. . .") the phrase occurs in 6:19 and, without *'al* and suffix, in 4:6: these two occurrences thus seem to function as an inclusio for the whole cycle proper, 4:5-6:30.

For the sake of completeness, mention should be made here of other variations of the pattern that may hold significance for our quest. One finds: (c) "behold I am bringing upon you a nation from afar" *(gôy mimmerḥaq)* in 5:15.[8] (d) Defined as *hinneh 'anî/'anokî* or *hin*e*nî* with *mebî' (ha)ra'â 'al/'el*, there are several occurrences of the phrase in the stereotyped prose—within chapters 1-20, in 11:11, 19:3 and 15.[9] (e) With a finite hiphil verb, before the end of chapter 20: 17:18, "bring upon them the day of evil."[10] (f) With a synonymous verb, before the end of chapter 20: 18:11, with the participle *yôṣer* in the narrative of the incident at the potter's house.[11]

I have already mentioned one occurrence of the phrase outside the book of Jeremiah—with qal verb, in Mic. 3:11; this passage then could well be one of the stimuli for the phrase in Jeremiah. On the other hand, the phrase, using a hiphil participle, seems to have been part of a standard old prophetic curse, occurring in 1 Kings 14:10 (Ahijah's judgment on the house of Jeroboam) and 21:21 Qr (Elijah's judgment on the house of Ahab). Both these passages contain the pungent idioms "he that pisses against the wall" and "bond and free" (or whatever *'aṣûr w*e*'azûb* means), and seem to be part of the traditional language of northern prophetic circles.[12] The phrase was continued in the diction of the Deuteronomic historian and in analogous material.[13]

In sum, we may conclude at this point that the old prophetic curse (with hiphil participle) and the passage in Micah (with qal) seem jointly to have stimulated both the phrase in Jer. 2:3 and the repetitions in 4:5-6:30. I shall examine the way the phrase functions in 4:5-6:30 at a later point.

There are other links between 2:3 and 4:5-30. One dramatic one is afforded by the verbl *'kl,* "eat," in contexts of destruction in war: the relevant parallel is 5:17, where the verb is repeated four times in a description of the foe from the north.[14] Another link is the word *l^{e}yhwh*, which reappears in 5:10: "Go up through her vine-rows and destroy. . .for they are not Yahweh's" (cf. 2:3: "Israel was holy to Yahweh"). Still another is the theme of first fruits of the harvest, which, as we shall see, is linked to references to the vineyard (5:10, 6:9). Since the parallels between 2:3 and 4:5-6:30 are so heavily concentrated in the passage 5:10-17, the question arises in our minds whether 5:10-17 is not in fact a *key section* in the foe cycle; I shall turn to this matter next (sections c and d).

In sum, just as we found that 2:2-3 offered cues to the structure of the harlotry cycle, so we may expect 2:2-3 to offer cues to the structure of the foe cycle.

c. The Harlotry Cycle and the Foe Cycle: Parallels and Contrasts

There is no question but that 4:5 begins something new: battle orders, cries for help; we are in a new world after the material in chapters 2-3 with their accent on sexuality. One curious way in which the contrast between the two cycles may be dramatized is statistically, in terms of the frequency of doubled consonants (*dagesh forte*). In reading the material in 4:5ff aloud, I was struck from time to time by the seeming frequency of doubled consonants, so that I took the trouble once to work out the pronunciation in Jeremiah's time of the consonants of the MT of chapters 2-3 and of 4:5-31, counting all doubled consonants, and working out the frequency of doubled consonants per 100 consonants of the written MT (including *matres lectionis*).[15] The frequency of doubled consonants in the 47 verses 2:2-3, 5-37, 3:1-5, 19-25 (vv. 24-25 reconstructed as I have done above, in 3,b) is 7.04%; the frequency of doubled consonants in the 26 verses 4:5-26, 28-31 is 10.1%.[16] In other words, the material in the foe cycle of chapter 4 offers 43% more geminated consonants than the material in the harlotry cycle of chapters 2-3. Acoustically, this contrast must have been quite striking; one cannot help wondering whether there were not other contrasts of rhythm, speed of delivery, tune, or gesture between the two corpora.

I have been noting contrasts between the two cycles, but there are likenesses as well. One is the striking likeness between 2:15 and 4:7, where the "lion" image seems to trigger similar diction:

2:15: *‘ālāyw̲ yiš’^{a}gû k^{e}p̄îrim*	Against/upon him roar the (young) lions,
nat̲^{e}nû qōlām̄	they give forth their voice,
wayyaš̲̂it̲û ’arṣô l^{e}šammâ	And they put (*šyt*) in his land to a waste,
‘arayw nis̲s^{e}tû (Qr)	his cities are burned (*yṣt*?),[17]
mibb^{e}li yošeb	without (*mibb^{e}lî*) inhabitant.
4:7: *‘ālâ ’aryeh missub̲b^{e}kô̲*	A lion has gone up from his thicket,
ûm̲a̲šḥît gôyim̲ nasa‘	and a destroyer of nations has set out,
yaṣa’ m̲imm^{e}qomô	has gone forth from his place,
laśûm̲ ’arṣek l^{e}šammâ	To put (*śym*) your land to a waste,
‘ar̲ayik tiṣṣénâ	your cities shall fall (*nṣh*),
me’ên yôšēb	without (*mibb^{e}lî*) inhabitant.

But there is an even more striking parallel, this time not of diction, but of structure within a single verse. The verse from the harlotry cycle (2:6) is part of the first section; the verse in the foe cycle is 5:15.

2:6	5:15
וְלֹא אָמְרוּ אַיֵּה יְהוָה	הִנְנִי מֵבִיא עֲלֵיכֶם
הַמַּעֲלֶה אֹתָנוּ מֵאֶרֶץ מִצְרָיִם	גּוֹי מִמֶּרְחָק
הַמּוֹלִיךְ אֹתָנוּ בַּמִּדְבָּר	בֵּית יִשְׂרָאֵל [נְאֻם־יְהוָה]
בְּאֶרֶץ עֲרָבָה וְשׁוּחָה	גּוֹי אֵיתָן הוּא
בְּאֶרֶץ צִיָּה וְצַלְמָוֶת	גּוֹי מֵעוֹלָם הוּא
בְּאֶרֶץ לֹא־עָבַר בָּהּ אִישׁ	גּוֹי לֹא־תֵדַע לְשֹׁנוֹ
וְלֹא־יָשַׁב אָדָם שָׁם׃	וְלֹא־תִשְׁמַע מַה־יְדַבֵּר׃

In both verses we have a hiphil participle of a verb of motion; in both, a noun (2:6 *'eres,* 5:15 *gôy*) if followed by other material, and then a threefold repetition of the same noun, in the last instance followed by $\bar{lo}$' and a verb, followed by $w^e\bar{lo}$' and a parallel verb. This congruence is not to my knowledge duplicated elsewhere in the book of Jeremiah. One wonders: were each of these verses sung to the same tune? Whatever may have been the manifestation of their likeness in Jeremiah's presentations, it is plain that we are in touch here in both verses with material that had great resonance. The second lines of each verse had antecedents. As for *hamma'aleh 'otanû me'eres misrayim,* it is an exact duplication of the narrative of the covenant at Shechem, Josh. 24:17, and the phrase is also found (with variation in the object pronoun) in Lev. 11:45 (P) and 2 Kings 17:7 (Deuteronomic historian); and of course, with other variations, the pattern appears again and again in the affirmation of God's saving acts (*e.g.,* Deut. 20:1). And *gôy memerhaq* has an antecedent in Isa. 5:26: the text there, *gwym mrhwq,* is surely to be emended to *gôy memerhaq* precisely on the basis of Jer. 5:15.[18] In both passages, then, Jeremiah is quoting "words of God" from the past, once when he moved Israel for Israel's saving, once when he moved a foreign power for Israel's undoing. *Heilsgeschichte* is for the moment at least to be replaced by *Unheilsgeschichte.* This congruence suggests not only a parity between the two verses, but a parity between the two cycles of material in which these verses appear: and, more, that 5:15 is in a location in the foe cycle (the nerve center, so to speak) analogous to the location of 2:6 within the harlotry cycle. For now we recall that the repetition of the verb *'kl* is in 5:17, and that two of the occurrences of the parallels to the phrase "evil came upon them" are found in 5:12 and 15. But if 2:5-13 is the first section of the harlotry cycle, does 5:10-17 have an analogous function in the foe cycle, in some way setting forth the theme, or serving as a nucleus? Why should one have to wait so long after 4:5 to get to the "heart of the matter"?

d. The Search for the Organizing Principle of the Foe Cycle

There is no question about it, it is not easy to find any basis of organization for the material in 4:5-6:30. One cannot proceed as one did for 2:5ff, taking the first unit of material as thematic for what follows. The first unit, 4:5-8, has no discernible relationship (of word, phraseology, theme, assonance) with what follows. We come upon battle orders, appeals to lament, and wisdom asides without obvious pattern, and no key words seem to obtrude themselves in the fashion we found for 2:5ff. But if no inner pattern is immediately apparent, neither is there any external pattern such as would be supplied by catchword links between oracles that are not organically related. And since we were drawn to 5:10-17 as a possible "nucleus," we shall have to be alert to other possibilities of organization for which the earlier material in the book has offered no parallel. Let us then take a closer look at 5:10-17.

Are vv. 10-17 a unit, or multiple?—or is the unit in question larger than 10-17? Let us begin at the end. The passage plainly ends at v. 17: vv. 18-19 are a secondary insertion, and v. 20 begins something new. But where does the unit begin? Verses 15-17 form a unity. Verse 14 seems linked to vv. 15-17 by more than the double occurrence of *hinᵉnî* (vv. 14, 15) and the double occurrence of *'kl* (vv. 14, 17): God's prophetic word to Jeremiah (v. 14) seems parallel to God's summons of the nation from afar. But the (false) prophets who are *rûaḥ* (v. 13) seem tied in by contrast to Jeremiah in v. 14; and those who speak falsely of Yahweh (v. 12) seem parallel to the (false) prophets in v. 13 (and this is true whether v. 13 embodies the words of the people—like the conclusion of v. 12—or of God or of Jeremiah); and the faithlessness of Israel in v. 11 is parallel to the false speaking of Yahweh in v. 12.

Can we work back to v. 10, then? The movement of thought from v. 10 to v. 11 is not immediately clear. Verse 10 offers images from the vineyard: the people (or someone, plural) are to root out (or at least prune) the vineyard (it is controverted whether the *'al* of the second colon is original or not), and the vineyard imagery is not continued in what follows. But it *is* picked up in "your vines and your fig trees" in v. 17, which suggests a kind of inclusio; and if we notice that v. 10 is a direct reversal of the imagery of 2:3,[19] then our growing realization that this passage is a central reflection of 2:3 will be confirmed. We have already noticed the link of *l^e^yhwh* between 2:3 and 5:10: in 2:3 we read, "Israel was holy to Yahweh (*qōdeš yiśrā'ēl l^e^yhwh*), the first-fruits of his harvest (*rē'šît t^e^bû'ātô*)"; in 5:10 we read, "Go up through her vine-rows and destroy. . . . for they are not Yahweh's (*kî lō' l^e^yhwh hēmmâ*)." Here is the reversal of the original relationship, so that the plants that produce the harvest must be rooted out. Evidently then, the "first fruits" image in 2:3 does not refer to a grain harvest, but to the vintage. The same imagery is reflected in Hos. 9:10, "Like grapes in the wilderness, I found Israel. Like the first fruit on the fig tree, in its first season (*b^e^rē'šîtāh*), I saw your fathers." It is also the imagery of the vineyard in Isa. 5:1-7.[20]

Verse 10 offers imperative plurals. So do vv. 20-21, where the next unit evidently begins. So do 4:5-6, which begins the whole cycle. Do imperative plurals mark the beginning of successive units in the cycle? It turns out that they do, and that an analysis of the material by means of the imperatives is an important step toward an understanding of the structure of the cycle.[21]

e. The Sections of the Foe Cycle

If we begin by listing all imperatives (not only the masculine plurals) and negative commands (*'al* plus second-person imperfects), we get the following list:

4:5—*haggîdû*
hašmî'û w^e^'imrû
(w^e^)tiq'û
qir'û mal'û
w^e^'imrû hē'ās^e^pû
4:6—*ś^e^'û*
hā'îzû 'al-ta'^a^mōdû
4:8—*ḥigrû*
sipdû w^e^hēlîlû
4:14—*kabb^e^sî*
4:16—*hazkîrû*
hašmî'û
5:1—*šôṭ^e^ṭû*
ûr^e^'û ûd^e^'û
ûbaqq^e^šû
5:10—*'^a^lû. . .w^e^saḥētû*

w<u>e</u>. . .('al-?)ta'ᵃśû	*hāšē<u>b</u>*
hasîrû	6:11—*sᵉpok*
5:20—*haggîdû*	6:16—*'imdû. . .ûrᵉ'û*
wᵉhašmî'ûhā	*wᵉša'ᵃlû*
sim'û	*ûlᵉkû*
6:1—*hā'îzû*	*wᵉmiṣ'û*
tiq'û	6:17—*haqšîbû*
śᵉ'û	6:18—*šim'û. . .ûdᵉ'î* (text?)
6:4—*qaddᵉšû*	6:19—*šim'î*
qûmû	6:25—*'al-tēṣᵉ'û/î*
6:5—*qûmû*	*'al-tēlēkû/î*
6:6—*kirtû. . .wᵉšipkû*	6:26—*ḥigrî*
6:8—*hiwwasᵉrî*	*wᵉhitpallᵉšî*
6:9—*'ôlēl yᵉ'ôlᵉlû* (text?)	*'ᵃśî.*

Now it becomes relatively simple to group the imperatives and use the groupings to delimit the sections of the foe cycle, because many of these imperatives are isolated. Thus we have already tentatively determined that 5:10 begins a section, and 5:20 another, and there are no other imperatives nearby. Neither are there around 5:1, which begins a section. Verse 6:1 makes a fresh start, in terminology reminiscent of 4:5-6; but here, in contrast to the isolated imperatives of 5:1, 5:10, and 5:20, we have imperatives that continue in a rather steady stream after 6:1, just as they do in 4:5ff. The way in which 6:1ff seems to return to the kind of material we have in 4:5ff suggests that 4:5-6:30 offers some kind of A-B-A' form. If then we examine the major themes of these emerging sections, their patterning falls into place: 6:9 reflects the kind of vineyard imagery that we found in 5:10; and 6:16 has wisdom motifs connected with "paths" (*dᵉrākîm*) reminiscent of the wisdom motifs of 5:1, which were connected with "streets" (*ḥûṣôt*). This leaves the long passage 4:5-31 as a single unit. Such an analysis yields seven sections in the form A-B-C-D-A'-C'-B':

A—4:5-31
    B—5:1-9
        C—5:10-17
            D—5:20-29
A'—6:1-8
        C'—6:9-15
    B'—6:16-30.

Such an analysis omits 5:30-31, which turns out to be a secondary addition; justification for this omission will be made below, 4, k. One might note that theoretically the "B" and "C" sections might be combined, and the "C' " and "B' " sections, making a division into five sections, the second and fifth of which would then offer a chiasmus; but considering the patterning of the imperatives already outlined, the sevenfold division seems best.

Once one has delimited these sections, many other details begin to leap to the eye. For example, in chapter 4 we have *bat-'ammî* in v. 11 and *bat-ṣiyyôn* in v. 31 (a kind of inclusio, after the initial subsection?), while in chapter 6 we have the two phrases in reverse order as vocatives, *bat-siyyôn* in v. 23 and *bat-'ammî* in v. 26 (a kind of inclusio for the penultimate subsection?). Again, both 4:5 and 6:27 offer *mbṣr* (4:5 *hammibṣār,* "fortification"; in 6:27 I suggest the vocalization *mibbōṣer,* "rather than a grape-gatherer." I shall justify this reading in 4, n. The occurrence of the same consonant cluster in 4:5 and 6:27 suggests that it is an inclusio; and when one sees, in 10:17, at the beginning of the last subdivision of the supplementary foe cycle, *bammāṣōr,* "under siege," for a new inclusio (see 6,c), he finds everything beginning to "fall into place."

Let us now take notice of a few more matters of form and content in the foe cycle. As to form, beyond the pattern of imperatives that begin each section, with which I have already dealt, the overriding impression gained by a reader or hearer as he proceeds through the cycle is that of the constant shifts of speaker (and audience as well, to some extent). These shifts sometimes cause the MT to stumble (*e.g.*, 6:17 *'ᵃlêkem* or, with two MSS., *'ᵃlêhem*; 6:25, where the verbs are feminine singular according to the Kt and masculine plural according to the Qr), or the commentators to emend, often wrongly from the perspective in the present study (*e.g.*, 5:1, where Rudolph earlier emended *wᵉ'eslaḥ* to *wᵉnislaḥ* "because the prophet is the speaker,"[22] but later changed his mind[23]). We shall find that *just as the imperatives helped delimit the major sections of the foe cycle, so that changes of speaker will help us to see structure within each individual section.*

As for content, there is a steady movement in each of the sections from battle scenes to wisdom preoccupations, so much so that the foe cycle might well be subtitled something like "The Battle That is Really a Pedagogical Device."

This movement is accomplished both in vocabulary and in structure. In vocabulary the link is made by verbs like "hear" and "see," and nouns like "heart": Jeremiah hears and sees the battle, so that his heart pounds (4:19-21), but the people cannot hear or see the necessities of obedience, because they have no heart (=sense) (5:21).

In the structure, one finds the movement from battle to wisdom on both a small and large scale. For example, in 4:13 we have the panicky thoughts of the inhabitants of Judah as the chariots come on upon them, and in the next verse we have an appeal (by God, or Jeremiah: we shall determine this later) to Jerusalem to "wash your heart from wickedness, that you may be saved." In vv. 19-21 of that chapter, we have Jeremiah's frantic thoughts as he visualizes the battle, and then in v. 22 the cool words of Yahweh the schoolmaster, that the people are foolish and have not learned to know him.[24] On the scale of the major sections of the cycle we move from the first (4:5-31), which is largely concerned with battle, to the second (5:1-9), in which the appeal is to "work through the streets of Jerusalem, to find an honest man." Indeed, there is inclusio *across the whole cycle* in such a movement from battle to wisdom: the first section, as we have noted, is concerned with battle, while the last section (6:16-30) is concerned with wisdom ("stand and look for the ancient paths"); note the ironic contrast of "do not stand" (*'al-ta'ᵃmodû*) (4:6) and "stand (still)" (*'imdû)* (6:16). Now, since the third subdivision (5:10-17) (and the sixth, 6:9-15) are concerned with the vineyard, moving the discussion in another direction, we begin to understand why the arrangement of the subdivisions is not a perfect chiasmus (A-B-C-D-C'-B'-A') or even a great A-B-A' form like (A-B-C)-D-(A'-B'-C'): if "A" is "battle" and "B" is "wisdom," and if the movement is from battle to wisdom, then we must end with wisdom—B'; and this being the case, the existing form, A-B-C-D-A'-C'-B' becomes the solution. (Question: The book of Deuteronomy has strong wisdom strands;[25] is Jeremiah here offering his own reflection on Deuteronomy?)[26]

All the imperatives sound like battle orders, but some of them turn into something else. Thus the imperatives in 4:5-6 are battle orders pure and simple; but the imperatives in 5:1, though they begin with the air of a search-and-destroy mission (*sôṭeṭû* sounds like "work through [the streets of Jerusalem] one by one),"[27] continue as wisdom ("see and know"). The imperatives in the next section, 5:10, sound at first like a rural analogue to the search-and-destroy of 5:1: "go up through her terraces" (parallel to "streets of Jerusalem" in 5:1) "and destroy," but this turns out, as we have seen, to be the destruction of the metaphorical vineyard, Israel. The fourth section, 5:20ff, begins with what could be a military announcement ("hear this"), but the whole section is a wisdom discourse. Then back to battle once more in the fifth section (6:1). The imperatives in 6:9 are of course agricultural, though *šwb* hiphil with the object *yad* may certainly be used in military contexts (*e.g.*, Amos 1:8). And the last section again begins with an imperative, which could well have been a battle command: *'md* in Nah. 2:9 seems to mean "halt," though its context in our passage, as we have seen, is wisdom. Thus we might title the sections as follows:

1. Battle Orders (4:5-31)
2. Orders that Turn Attention to Wisdom (5:1-9)
3. Metaphorical Orders, to Destroy the Vineyard Israel (5:10-17)
4. The "Lesson" of Yahweh the Schoolmaster (5:20-29)
5. Again Battle Orders (6:1-8)
6. Again Metaphorical Orders, to Glean the Vineyard Israel (6:9-15)
7. Again Orders that Turn Attention to Wisdom (6:16-30).

Now we can begin to understand how it is that the first section, 4:5ff, did not offer key words and phrases for later sections of the cycle, as 2:5ff did for the earlier cycle. The first section of the harlotry cycle (2:5-13) was the description of Israel's plight and of Yahweh's indictment of her. But the message of the foe cycle is that the coming battle is really a pedagogical device. This is a surprise, something that takes some time to unfold. One does not ordinarily think of a battle as a pedagogical device: a battle is a battle. But this battle is different, and the true meaning of the battle only becomes apparent as one works into the material: Isaiah did the same thing on a smaller scale when he offered the Song of the Vineyard (Isa. 5:1-7)—again the vineyard!—and only revealed the identity of the vineyard and of the husbandman at the end. So here, it takes awhile. No wonder the links with the seed oracle (2:2-3), and a verse congruent with 2:6, are not found until the third section, as we discovered some time ago: here the ultimate theme or nucleus is not at the beginning; rather, the secret is made plain toward the center, just before Yahweh's lecture.

One more observation before I begin to analyze the material section by section, and that concerns the patterning of length and complexity of the sections. The first section is far longer than the others. If as a rough indication of length I list the number of verses (in the MT) of each section, we obtain:

First Section (4:5-31) — 27 verses
Second Section (5:1-9) — 9 verses
Third Section (5:10-17) — 8 verses
Fourth Section (5:20-29) — 10 verses
Fifth Section (6:1-8) — 8 verses
Sixth Section (6:9-15) — 7 verses
Seventh Section (6:16-30) — 15 verses.

The first section, as we shall see, is complex and is best divided into five subsections; the second, third, fifth, and sixth sections all turn out to be of a simple A-B-A' type with strong unity; the fourth and central section breaks easily into two halves; and the seventh and last section is in three subsections, each rather a unit in itself. There is a symmetry here by which the first and last sections balance each other in complexity, and since the last section contains reminiscences of much of the earlier material, it manifests a common phenomenon in Jeremiah's poetry by which a closing unit summarizes all that has come before.[28]

Now we must examine the sections one by one.

f. The First Section: Battle Orders (4:5-31); Basic Structure

If it was not easy to delimit the sections of the foe cycle and understand their relationship, it is not easy to work out the full structure of the first (and longest) section, either. In general we find direct descriptions of battle scenes in vv. 5-7, 13, 15-17, and 29; that is to say, the battle descriptions are in three areas of the passage: the beginning, the middle, and the end. The battle descriptions are filled out in these three areas by related material that offers a reaction to the battle, or a reason for the battle (vv. 8, 14, 18, 30-31), so that the three battle scenes make up vv. 5-8, 13-18, and 29-31. Between the battle scenes are two double interludes: the first double interlude (vv. 9-12) introduced by "in that day" (*bayyôm hahû'*) (v. 9) and "at that time" (*bā'ēt hahî'*) (v. 11), the second double interlude (vv. 19-28) offering two inner experiences of Jeremiah—the uproar of his inner organs (vv. 19-21) and his vision of cosmic chaos (vv. 23-26).

This fivefold division, which I posit from a superficial survey, is confirmed by the symmetry of several key words. The first half of the first double interlude offers the two parallel nouns, *lēb* and *nepeš:* "the *lēb* of the king, the *lēb* of the princes shall fail" (thus twice in v. 9), and "the sword has reached their very *nepeš*" (v. 10). The second half offers the assonantal pair *midbār* and (the verb) *dibbēr:* "a hot wind. . .in the desert" (v. 11), and "now it is I who speak ('ᵃ*dabbēr*) judgment upon them" (v. 12). (The association of these two is found previously in 3:2 [*midbār*] and 3:5 [*dibbart*], and possibly in 2:31 [*dᵉbar*, if the text is correct, and *midbār*].) Then the second double interlude offers precisely the same four words in the same order: the first half again has *lēb* twice, followed by *nepeš* (all in v. 19: *libbi, libbi, napši*), while the second half has *midbār* (v. 26) and *dibbartî* (v. 28). Furthermore, the *second battle scene* has *lēb* in an inclusio (vv. 14, 18: *libbēk* twice), and the *third battle scene* has *nepeš* twice (v. 30, *napšēk;* v. 31, *napšî).* Finally, the battle scenes themselves are united by common vocabulary: *'lh*, "go up," in vv. 7, 13; *qôl* in vv. 15, 16 (and 19, 21), 29, and 31 twice; and by the animal imagery—"lion," v. 7, "horses swifter than eagles," v. 13; and perhaps we may include "horseman," v. 29.

We have, then, the following outline:

a. The First Battle Scene (vv. 5-8)
b. The First Double Interlude:
   (i) (vv. 9-10) — *lēb* twice, *nepeš*
   (ii) (vv. 11-12) — *midbār,* 'ᵃ*dabbēr*
c. The Second Battle Scene (vv. 13-18) — *libbēk* in inclusio vv. 14, 18
d. The Second Double Interlude:
   (i) (vv. 19-22) — *libbî* twice, *napšî*
   (ii) (vv. 23-28) — *midbār, dibbartî*
e. The Third Battle Scene (vv. 29-31) — *napšēk* v. 30, *napšî* v. 31.

We sense that not only are the battle scenes related to

each other, and the interludes to each other, by shared vocabulary and key words, but the interludes are related to the battle scenes as well. For example, in v. 18 we hear that disaster (*rā'â*—an echo of v. 6) has reached the very heart (*nāga' 'ad-libbēk*), a phrase that not only echoes v. 14 in an inclusio (*kabbᵉsi mērā'â libbēk*, "wash your heart from wickedness") but also v. 10 (*wᵉnāgᵉ'ā ḥereb 'ad-hannepeš*). (We may note in passing that these phrases offer a good example of how battle concerns—v. 10—move to wisdom concerns—v. 14.)

A more striking example of a sharing of phraseology between interlude and battle scene is offered by the second double interlude—what Jeremiah sees and hears; the phraseology here echoes material from both of the first two battle scenes, and *in almost exact order of the material in those battle scenes*. This can best be shown in the following scheme:

Second Interlude	*First Battle Scene*	*Second Battle Scene*
"sound of trumpet" inclusio vv. 19, 21	"trumpet" v. 5	
šeber v. 20	*šeber* v. 6	
šuddᵉdâ v. 20		*šuddādnû* v. 13
"how long must I see the standard" v. 21	"standard" v. 6	"how long" v. 14
"cities laid in ruins" (*ntṣ* niphal) v. 26	"cities fall" (*nṣh* qal) v. 7	
"before Yahweh, before his fierce anger" v. 26	"the fierce anger of Yahweh" v. 8.	

The only items out of order are *šeber* and "standard" within v. 6.

The last battle scene brings a fresh pair of images, that of the painted woman and that of the woman in travail. In a way the image of the painted woman is a throwback to images of harlotry in the harlotry cycle, but the theme of the woman in travail is a standard one for panic in holy war,[29] and the phrase *qôl kᵉḥôlâ šāma'tî* has been prepared for by words in the second interlude, v. 19, where the word *'ôḥîlâ* (or whatever; the vocalization is uncertain), *qôl,* and *šāma'tî* appear. (We recall the inclusio of *qôl* and *šm'* in the last section of chapter 3.)

In sum, the first section offers us a most satisfactory symmetrical structure in themes and words. But the identification of the various speakers in this section proves to be a far more difficult task, and it is to this task that we now turn.

g. The First Section: The Search for the Identity of the Speakers

We have already taken note of the impression given, in the foe cycle, of sudden changes in the identity of speaker and audience. These changes seem particularly frequent in this first section. The problem, of course, is to isolate the kind of clues that can lead to some certainty in their identification; and not only are such clues fewer than we desire, but I suspect that the task is made more difficult in that Jeremiah often allows different speakers to mimic each other.

The identification of speakers in the interludes occasions no particular difficulty. The material in the first interlude (vv. 9-12) is specifically marked as to speaker: v. 9 has *nᵉ'um-yhwh*, and whether that rubric is original or not, there would be so reason to deny the attribution here; v. 10 ("Then I said, 'Ah Lord Yahweh, surely thou hast utterly deceived this people' ") is just as obviously spoken by Jeremiah, and vv. 11-12 are again the words of Yahweh (v. 12, "it is I who speak in judgment"). The material in the second double interlude is also clear. Verse 22 is spoken by God ("they know me not"), while the words of vv. 19-21 are inconceivable in any other mouth than Jeremiah's. Specifically, if we lay v. 22 alongside vv. 19-21, we find the ironic assonantal mimicry of *'ammî,* "my people" (v. 22), after *mē'ay,* "my bowels" (v. 19), reinforced, perhaps, by *'ᵉwîl* (v. 22) after *'ōhālay* (v. 20) and by *hāra'* and *yādā'û* (v. 22) after *yᵉrî'ōtay* (v. 20); and we sense, too, that complete contrast of emotional level between vv. 19-21 and v. 22: vv. 19-21 tell what Jeremiah's *nepeš* "hears" (v. 19). In parallel fashion vv. 23-26 tell what Jeremiah sees (note "Yahweh" in the third person in v. 26), and vv. 27-28 are spoken by Yahweh (evidenced not only by the rubric *kî kōh 'āmar yhwh* in v. 27, but also by the first-person verbs in vv. 27-28).[30]

It is in the sorting out of the material in the three battle scenes that we find the major difficulty in identification of speakers; these are a real Chinese puzzle, where each detail seems to depend upon some other detail. As a matter of fact, earlier commentators, faced with the confusing changes of speaker, have often resorted to theories of the *blending of voices*—where the "I" of God and the "I" of Jeremiah are identified,[31] or even where God and the people are identified.[32] But I have found it best to keep the voices quite distinct; we shall find, I think, that the rhetorical patterns can be understood satisfactorily without resort to any theory of blending.

Let us begin by laying, alongside the three battle scenes in this first section, one more—the final battle scene in the last section, namely, 6:22-26 (which I shall call in the present analysis the *fourth battle scene).* These four belong together—various groupings of them share a variety of features. Thus the first and fourth share a description of battle horrors, followed by an appeal in imperatives to lament, followed by a quotation (with "us") expressing the panic of the people:

battle horrors:

4:7: A lion has gone up
from his thicket,
a destroyer of nations
has set out;
he has gone forth from
his place
to make your land a
waste;
your cities will fall,
without inhabitant.

6:25: Go not forth into the
field,
nor walk on the road;
for the enemy has a
sword,
terror is on every
side.

appeal to lament:

4:8a: For this gird you
with sackcloth,
lament and wail,

6:26a: O daughter of my people, gird on sackcloth, and roll in
ashes;
make mourning as for
an only son, most
bitter lamentation;

panic of the people:

4:8b: For the fierce anger
of Yahweh has not
turned back from us

6:26b: For suddenly the
destroyer will come
upon us.

The second and third battle scenes also contain an expression of panic—toward the beginning of the second (4:13) and the end of the third (4:31): 4:13 has *'ôy lānû,* and 4:31 has its assonantal reverse, *'ôy-nā' lî:*

4:13b — Woe to us *('ôy lānû),*
for we are ruined.

4:31b — Woe is me *('ôy-nā' lî),*
for I am fainting before
murderers.

Two more parallels among these scenes may be noted: the second and the fourth, in the statements of panic, have *šdd,* "ruin" (4:13b, 6:26b); and the third and fourth have references to a woman in travail (4:31, 6:24).

In spite of such variety of pairings as is possible among these four, it becomes plain that there is a particularly close likeness between the second and the fourth:

4:13a — battle description	parallel to 6:22-23
4:13b — reference to "us" and use of *šdd*	parallel to 6:26b
4:14 — fem. sing. vocative, appeal to repentance	parallel to 6:26a
4:15-17 — battle description, use of *sabîb*	parallel to 6:25.

We are left with only one verse in each passage that has no parallel in the other, namely, 4:18 and 6:24. The inverse order of the parallels between 4:13b-17 and 6:25-26, and the general similarity of the imagery, will lead us to analyze the patterning of the speakers of these two passages side by side; but I will postpone analyzing them for the moment, since they are the more complex pair, to deal with the simpler pair, the two remaining—4:5-8 and 4:29-31.

When we look at 4:5-8, the first thing we notice is that we find "I" in v. 6 (the speaker is obviously Yahweh) but "Yahweh" and "us" in v. 8. Volz and Rudolph get us partway to a solution by their suggestion that the *kî* clause in v. 8 gives the *content of the lamentation* to which the people are to give voice; that is, v. 8 must be read, ". . . lament and wail, 'The fierce anger of Yahweh has in no way turned back from us!' "[33] This suggestion brings 4:8b into parallelism with 4:31b—in both cases we have a quotation of the people, referred to in the first-person plural in 4:8b and in the singular in 4:31b.

But I do not take the appeal to lament in v. 8a as an

appeal voiced by Yahweh, but rather as an appeal voiced by Jeremiah. I am led to this conclusion by several lines of thinking. One general consideration is that among the traditional functions of a prophet is that of calling the people to repentance (*e.g.*, Jer. 25:5 and often); so to assign v. 8 to Jeremiah would be to see him fulfilling that function here. But there are more specific considerations.

(1) Mic. 1:6-8 is closely parallel to Jer. 4:7-8. Now, in Mic. 1:6-7 God speaks, and the diction is very similar to that of Jer. 4:7—thus Mic. 1:6 describes how Samaria shall become a heap in the open country, and Jer. 4:7 mentions that "your cities will fall."[34] Then Mic. 1:8 begins with *'al-zō't,* and it is clear that the speaker is the prophet, urging himself to lament and wail (*'espᵉdâ wᵉ'ēlîlâ*); and Jer. 4:8 likewise begins with *'al-zōt*, and we find here plural imperatives to lament and wail *(sipdû wᵉhêlîlû)*. This similarity would suggest that it is Jeremiah who speaks in 4:8. Conceivably another solution is possible: in Jer. 4:8 God could continue to be the speaker, urging the people (imperative plurals) to lament as a response to what he has announced in vv. 5-7, just as Micah's urge to lament in Mic. 1:8 was his response to what God had announced in 1:6; but the pattern of change of speaker between Mic. 1:6 and 1:8 is at least suggestive.

(2) We have seen that there is a curious parallel of phraseology between 4:7-8 and the last part of the second interlude, 4:26, 28: vv. 7 and 26 speak of cities in ruins, using different (though assonantally echoing) verbs;[35] but now we notice that vv. 8 and 28 both begin with *'al-zō't* and that the topic in both verses concerns mourning.

v. 7 — your cities will fall (*'arayik tiṣṣênâ* [*nṣh* qal])	v. 26 — all its cities were laid in ruins (*kol-'arayw nittᵉṣû* [*nts* niphal])[36]
v. 8 — for this (*'al-zō't*) gird on sackcloth, lament and wail	v. 28 — for this (*'al-zō't*) the earth shall mourn, and the heavens above be black.[37]

But there is a shift of speaker from v. 26 to v(v. 27-) 28, from Jeremiah to God; this sequence here could well be an echo of vv. 7-8, with a change in the other direction, from God to Jeremiah.

(3) If *vv. 26 and 28* in the second interlude imitate the diction of the *first battle scene,* then (symmetrically) the *third battle scene* imitates the diction of *v. 19* in the second interlude: v. 31 *kî qôl kᵉḥôlâ šāma'tî* echoes v. 19 *kî qôl šôpār šāma't(î) napšî;* and since v. 19 is spoken by Jeremiah, v. 31 with its quotation is pretty clearly spoken by Jeremiah, suggesting then by symmetry that v. 8 is likewise spoken by him.

(4) There is a symmetry with 6:26, with its appeal to gird on sackcloth and mourn, as we have seen. The vocative there, *bat-'ammî,* makes the conclusion almost inevitable that Jeremiah speaks that verse,[38] and symmetry with 4:8 leads us to the conclusion that Jeremiah speaks this one as well.

The last clear indication in the first battle scene that Yahweh is speaking is in 4:6 ("I bring evil from the north"), but considerations (1) and (2) above suggest by analogy that he continues to speak in v. 7. Verse 8 will then be spoken by Jeremiah and ends with his hypothetical quotation of the people's expression of panic. We have, then:

4:5-7 — Yahweh's description of the battle

4:8a — Jeremiah's appeal to the people to lament
4:8b — Jeremiah's hypothetical quotation of the people's lament.

Let us now deal with the other battle scene of this pair, namely, the third battle scene, 4:29-31. There are not too many direct clues here. It has already been established (consideration 3 above) that Jeremiah speaks v. 31, ending with a quotation of the people's expression of their plight. There are few direct clues to identify the speaker(s) in vv. 29 and 30. One has the impression of a change of viewpoint between v. 30 (people addressed as second-person-singular feminine, image of painted woman) and v. 31 (people referred to in the third-person-singular feminine, image of woman in travail). Verse 29 contains a battle description analogous to that of vv. 5-7, where Yahweh was the speaker; and though there is no absolute necessity that Yahweh be the speaker in v. 29 as he was in vv. 5-7, simplicity suggests that, lacking evidence to the contrary, we so assign the verse. Verse 30 would also be best understood in the mouth of Yahweh: the tone fits the general outlook of 3:1-5 and other such passages. And there is one more clue that the change of speaker comes between v. 30 and v. 31 (*i.e.,* that v. 30 be assigned to Yahweh, since we know that v. 31 is to be assigned to Jeremiah), and this clue, again, is found in the parallel in 6:24-26. For the "travail" image occurs once more, in 6:24, where the speaker is plainly the people ("we," "us"). The image is followed in 6:26 by a parallel image, the woman bereaved of her only son. But we have already seen that 6:26 is to be assigned to Jeremiah (consideration 4 above); this transition suggests a parallel change of speaker between the two images of women in 4:30-31. The two passages may be laid side by side, as follows:

4:30 — God's address to the people as a painted woman	
4:31 — Jeremiah's description of the people in panic as a woman in travail	6:24 — the people's expression of helplessness as a woman in travail
	6:26 — Jeremiah's appeal to the people as a mother bereft of her son.

With good probability, then, the speakers are identified as follows:

4:29 — Yahweh's description of the battle
4:30 — Yahweh's address to the people as a painted woman
4:31a — Jeremiah's description of the people in panic as a woman in travail
4:31b — Jeremiah's quotation of the people's cry of panic.

Understood in this way, 4:29-31, the last subsection of the first section forms a complete parallel to 4:5-8, the first subsection.

So much for the first and third battle scenes. Now let us turn to the other pair, the second (4:13-18) and fourth (6:22-26). I have already made a few assignments in the fourth scene—6:24 to the people, 6:26a to Jeremiah. Now if 6:26a belongs to Jeremiah, then the *kî* clause in v. 26b is entirely analogous to the *kî* clause in 4:8b—a quotation in which Jeremiah gives voice to the hypothetical lamentation of the people.[39] Verse 26 is then analogous to 4:8:

6:26a — Jeremiah's appeal to the people
6:26b — Jeremiah's hypothetical quotation of the people's lament.

Let us next consider 4:13. Here again, the last half of the verse contains an interjection of panic from the people, and given the analogies of 4:31b and 6:26b, we can have no hesitation in assigning 4:13b to the people. As for 4:13a, theoretically it could be spoken by anyone, but I think almost inevitably this material must be assigned to Yahweh. It is analogous to 6:22-23 (each begins with *hinnēh,* and each has a reference to horses). The material in 6:22-23 is introduced by *kōh 'āmar yhwh,* and whether or not this rubric is original, I think it is trustworthy, for in the passage we find a recapitulation of the initial battle description of 4:5-7 ("north," "great"), and a contemptuous address to the daughter of Zion reminiscent of 4:30. Further, if we assign 4:13a to Yahweh and 4:13b to the people, we have a miniature parallel to the first battle scene (without the word from Jeremiah). Therefore this identification is indicated:

4:13a — Yahweh's description of the battle
4:13b — the people's cry of panic.

Verses 14 and 18 of chapter 4 balance: the address to Jerusalem is feminine singular, the use of "heart" in a wisdom sense; they are in contrast to vv. 15-17, where the feminine-singular references are in the third person (v. 17 twice). Verse 17 further identifies the speaker as Yahweh. The contrast between vv. 15-17 on the one hand, and vv. 14 and 18 on the other, strongly suggests that vv. 15-17 as a whole be assigned to Yahweh, while vv. 14 and 18 be assigned to Jeremiah, who appeals to the people to repent as he did in v. 8a. We would have, then, a basic alternation (Yahweh, Jeremiah, Yahweh, Jeremiah) in vv. 13-18, with the short interjection from the people in 13b to interrupt; in this way all of the speakers of vv. 5-8 speak again, but the patterning is somewhat enlarged:

4:13a — Yahweh's description of the battle

4:13b — the people's cry of panic
4:14 — Jeremiah's appeal to the people to repent
4:15-17 — Yahweh's description of the battle
4:18 — Jeremiah's explanation to the people of the meaning of the battle.

This patterning solves virtually all the assignments in 6:22-26: vv. 22-23 are spoken by Yahweh, v. 24 by the people; v. 26 is spoken by Jeremiah, with a final cry from the people. But what about v. 25? Here the tradition is uncertain: the Kt reads feminine-singular imperatives, which would identify the material with v. 26, which likewise offers a feminine-singular imperative (suggesting then that Jeremiah is speaking); the Qr reads masculine plurals, which would identify the imperatives with the battle imperatives of a great deal of the whole cycle 4:5-6:30, suggesting then that Yahweh is speaking (as in 4:5-6). The question then becomes: what is the basic imagery of the verbs in v. 25?—are they battle orders, or appeals to repentance? We have seen that they have to do with battle ("Go not forth in the field" is synonymous with "Assemble and let us go into the fortified cities," 4:5, and "nor walk on the road" is synonymous with "stand by on the roads," 6:16), hence the Qr (and Versions) must be read, and Yahweh is the speaker. Therefore we have:

6:22-23 — Yahweh's description of the battle
6:24 — the people's expression of helplessness
6:25 — Yahweh's battle orders
6:26a — Jeremiah's last-ditch appeal to the people to repent
6:26b — Jeremiah's hypothetical quotation of the people's lament.

The symmetry of these four battle scenes is satisfying, and we seem to have identified a self-consistent set of voices, without resorting to any theories of blending and without any voice's being "out of character." Other solutions may be possible, but I have not found them.

Let us now sum up the first section:

First Battle Scene:	vv. 5-7 — Yahweh's description of the battle v. 8a — Jeremiah's appeal to the people v. 8b — Jeremiah's hypothetical quotation of the people's lament
First Interlude:	v. 9 — general statement (tagged with n^{e}*'um-yhwh*) v. 10 — Jeremiah ("and I said") vv. 11-12 — Yahweh ("it will be said" — implication: by Yahweh)
Second Battle Scene:	13a — Yahweh's description of the battle v. 13b — the people's cry of panic v. 14 — Jeremiah's appeal to the people to repent vv. 15-17 — Yahweh's description of the battle v. 18 — Jeremiah's explanation to the people of the meaning of the battle
Second Interlude:	vv. 19-21 — long speech by Jeremiah: what he has heard (and seen) v. 22 — Yahweh's short reply vv. 23-26 — long speech by Jeremiah: what he has seen v(v. 27-)28 — Yahweh's short reply
Third Battle Scene:	vv. 29-30 — Yahweh's description of the battle, and address to

the people as a painted woman
v. 31a — Jeremiah's description of the people in panic as a woman in travail
v. 31b — Jeremiah's quotation of the people's cry of panic.

h. The Second Section: Orders that Turn Attention to Wisdom (5:1-9)

The second section picks up the verb *biqqēš* (5:1, twice) from 4:30 and begins a new series of imperatives. The first one, as we have already seen, could well be heard as a battle order ("Work through the streets of Jerusalem"), but the next imperatives are wisdom ones ("and see and know," cf. 4:21, 22) and the rest of the section continues with strong wisdom motifs. There is symmetry within the section (*slḥ*, "pardon," vv. 1 and 7, *šbʿ* niphal, "swear," in reference to false swearing vv. 2 and 7, and *nkh* hiphil vv. 3 and 6), while the battle descriptions in 5:6 are reminiscent of those in 4:7 ("lion," "cities"). We are reminded of what we have already discovered: that 5:2 and 3 offer the parallels for the prelude (4:1-4) and the postlude (8:4-10a, 13); this is perhaps a way of suggesting to the hearer that one is getting now more into the heart of the matter under discussion: the battle is a *lesson* to the people.

It is a fairly simple matter to identify the speaker and audience in the verses of this section. Yahweh obviously speaks in v. 1 ("that I may pardon her").[40] Verses 4 and 5 are just as plainly spoken by Jeremiah; this material attracts v. 3 to it (vocative to Yahweh, speaking about "them" as in vv. 4 and 5) and v. 2 as well ("they"); v. 2 is in contrast to v. 1, where the third-person reference is to a feminine singular. The speaker in vv. 7-9 is just as plainly Yahweh again ("how can I pardon you?"). Verse

6 moves rhetorically in the orbit of what follows rather than what precedes: the transition word *'al-ken* then fulfills the same function as did *'al-zo't* in 4:8.[41] Therefore we have:

v. 1 — Yahweh's mock battle orders about Jerusalem
vv. 2-5 — Jeremiah's testimony about the people who are ignorant
vv. 6-9 — Yahweh's description of the punishment to come.

We note the nice symmetry by which Yahweh in v. 1 is talking to the audience in the masculine plural about "her," while in vv. 6-9 he is talking to the audience in the feminine singular about "them" (=your [fem. sing.] apostate children).

The battle scenes and the wisdom motifs were rather distinctly contrasted in the first section; here, we find, they are blended.

i. The Third Section: Metaphorical Orders, to Destroy the Vineyard Israel (5:10-17)

If the second section had a couple of reflections of the prelude and postlude, the third section has steady reflections of 2:3, as we have already noted. The tension is rising! In the preliminary survey we saw how "go up through her terraces and destroy" is a rural parallel to "work through the streets of Jerusalem" in 5:1, but just as 5:1 offered an order that turns to wisdom, so the order here turns out to be metaphorical: the vineyard imagery (implied by "her terraces" and confirmed by *n^eṭîšôtéha,* "her tendrils," and the bald statement *lo' l^eyhwh hemmâ,* reversing 2:3,[42] makes it clear that we have a metaphorical reference to judgment on Israel, the erstwhile first fruits of Yahweh's harvest.

A major problem is whether *'al* in v. 10 is original or not. There are good arguments on both sides. If the imagery of v. 10 centers around *pruning,* then the *'al* may stand. If the material in 6:9ff is to be considered subsequent to or consequent on 5:10ff, then "remnant of Israel" in 6:9 would imply pruning in 5:10 and a thorough harvest in 6:9ff. On the other hand, it is arguable that the relationship between these sections is thematic rather than historical-sequential, so that the previous argument would not carry weight. The wording of the end of the section, 5:17, is one of thorough destruction: the verb *šḥt* piel certainly implies it (cf. 12:10). On balance, it seems best to omit the *'al* (with Rudolph, against Bright), seeing its presence as a mitigating gloss like (at least the *lō'* of) 4:27.[43]

Who are the participants in this dialogue? The parallel to 5:10 in the sixth section is 6:9—there the speaker can only be Yahweh, addressing Jeremiah. Since all of the other imperatives have been spoken by Yahweh, one assumes that he is speaking here, in spite of the third-person reference *kî lō' lᵉyhwh hēmmâ* in the last line of v. 10: v. 11 is plainly spokely by Yahweh, and the *kî* introducing the verse would scarcely introduce a change of speaker. The third-person reference in v. 10 can be explained only as a parallel to 2:3, where the same phraseology appears. (Another thought: if the commands in 5:10 are addressed to the enemy—so also Volz, Rudolph—would this make Yahweh's reference to himself in the third person more likely?)

The speaker is clearly Jeremiah in v. 12, and by implication in v. 13, which is closely linked to it: it is the false prophets who keep saying, "no evil shall come upon us" (cf. 23:17).[44]

The speaker is just as clearly Yahweh in vv. 14-17: he addresses Jeremiah in v. 14, and the nation in vv. 15-17, as the doom is pronounced.

The sequence of speakers that we find here—Yahweh,

Jeremiah, Yahweh—then matches the sequence in the second section.

j. The Fourth Section: The "Lesson" of Yahweh the Schoolmaster (5:20-29)

We are here at the geometrical midpoint of the seven-part cycle, the central section that has no counterpart between the beginning and the end.[45] The passage is a "lesson" by Yahweh the schoolmaster, and there is no necessity to assume any change of speaker: Yahweh speaks from beginning to end, and in this respect also this section stands alone in the cycle. The material starts out just as 4:5 did, with "declare. . . , proclaim. . . ," but instead of emergency battle orders, we are enjoined to listen to the wisdom-discourse of Yahweh. No, there are no battle noises here at all, and the quiet lesson is the greatest possible contrast, a contrast only briefly anticipated in 4:22. But it is the quiet of the eye of a hurricane. If the tension was rising from the second to the third section, it is in a way now at a peak, precisely because the midpoint, without counterpart, gains the maximum attention. Yahweh states the real reason for the destruction now about to be visited upon the nation, and the discourse is heavy with occurrences of *lēb* (vv. 21, 23, 24), *r'h* (v. 21), *šm'* (v. 20, 21 twice).

Structurally, the section breaks into two parts: vv. 21-24 with *lēb* and *ḥōq* (vv. 22, 24), and vv. 25-29 with the inclusio of *'ēlleh* (vv. 25, 29) and possibly the words *rᵉšā'îm* (v. 26) and *rā'* (v. 28). The two parts are held together by the verb *'br* (vv. 22, 28) and by the assonance *gᵉbûl*, "bound" (v. 22), and *kᵉlûb*, "basket" (v. 27), two words that help to generate the two images of the boundary of the sea and the basket of birds. The two subsections also have a symmetry in references to the erring people: vv. 20-22 have the second-person plural, vv. 23-24 the third person; v. 25 the second-person plural, and vv. 26-29 the third person again.

I suggested a moment ago that the calm of this section was the calm of the eye of a hurricane. This figure of speech was not offered casually, because behind the words are assonances reminiscent of the battle scenes. For example, in v. 22 we have *ḥôl*, "sand," which reminds us of *'ōḥilâ* (or whatever the original vocalization was) in the reaction of Jeremiah's inner organs in 4:19, and of *ḥôlâ*, the woman in travail in 4:31; again, in 5:22 we have *ḥōq-'ôlām,* "perpetual barrier," which remind us of the parallelism describing the foe from the north in 5:15 as a nation *mimmerḥāq, mē'ôlām*! (We are reminded of the assonantal contrast *'ammî, mē'ay* in 4:22 and 19 between Yahweh and Jeremiah.)[46]

The parallels with earlier sections are more than assonantal; they are structural as well. As v. 20 imitates the beginning of the first section (4:5), so v. 29 replicates the end of the second section (5:29=5:9). Structurally, then, the third and fourth sections in their contrasting ways state the issue on the cosmic level: the covenant with Yahweh has been broken, so that Yahweh is reversing the initial honeymoon status of the people and he calls Jeremiah to announce that the enemy will devour the nation successfully (2:3, and the third section, 5:10-17); then Yahweh himself lectures the people on their obtuseness and implies what covenant loyalty should be (the present section), material that in format replicates the first section (battle) and the second section (wisdom) and puts them in perspective.

k. A Short Inserted Oracle (5:30-31)

These two verses are intrusive, and break the outline I am presenting. I made the suggestion some years ago[47] that the curious phrase *yirdû ‘al-y^{e}dêhem* in v. 31 is an *ad hoc* antonym for *millē’ ’et-y^{e}dêhem*, the normal formula for the consecration of a priest. I now reinforce that suggestion by proposing that the two verses are lodged here precisely because of that association, for the root *ml’* appears twice in v. 27. This is not an association by catchword, since *ml’* does not appear in vv. 30-31, but its antonym does; it is more like the practice of "adjunction by preexisting association," several examples of which will be found in later chapters.[48]

l. The Fifth Section: Again Battle Orders (6:1-8)

With the fifth section we are back to battle scenes again, in material parallel to that of the first section. The second and third sections each offered a simple three-part exchange—Yahweh, Jeremiah, Yahweh—while the fourth was a monologue of Yahweh's. The first section offered a whole complex of interchanges in which the people as well as Yahweh and Jeremiah took part; is this the case here? It is, though of course on a more modest scale, since the present section is only eight verses long; but the center-point is a rapid exchange—enemy, people, enemy (vv. 4-5)—where the people's "woe to us" is an echo of the same expression in 4:13. The text of v. 2 should probably be emended to "Hast thou become a meadow lovely, O daughter of Zion?" (so Bright); "daughter of Zion" is a vocative in 6:23, and v. 8 has a vocative, "Jerusalem" to balance it (note also the vocative "Jerusalem" in 4:14.[49] There is no reason, then, to assume any other speaker for vv. 1-3, 6-8 except Yahweh. The symmetry is really most appealing:

(A)	v. 1 — Yahweh to Judah (masc. pl.)		about the enemy
(B)	v. 2 — Yahweh to dau.-Zion (fem. sg.)		
(C)	v. 3 — Yahweh		about the enemy and about "her"
(D)	v. 4a — enemy to enemy		about "her"
	v. 4b — Judah		
	v. 5 — enemy to enemy		about "her"
(A')	v. 6 — Yahweh to enemy (masc. pl.)		about Jerus.
(C')	v. 7 — Yahweh		about "her"
(B')	v. 8 — Yahweh to Jerus. (fem. sg.)		

So analyzed, in fact, the structure of this section is exactly that of the overall structure of the foe cycle: A-B-C-D-A'-C'-B'. (Note also that this is an elaboration of a similar symmetry in the second section [5:1, 6-9]: see the discussion above.)

The word linkages with the first section are very close, as we might expect: v. 1 is a close variation of 4:5b-6 (as the beginning of the fourth section was a close variation of 4:5a); *sābîb* (6:3) is found in 4:17, and *našḥîtâ* in 6:5 mimics *mašḥît* in 4:7. And one wonders whether the uniting sound-sequence *ḥol-* (4:19, 31, 5:22) is not picked up once more here in *ḥᵒlî* (6:7).

m. The Sixth Section: Again Metaphorical Orders, to Glean the Vineyard Israel (6:9-15)

If Yahweh has addressed metaphorical vineyard commands to the enemy in the third section (5:10), and if Yahweh has addressed concrete battle commands to the enemy in the fifth section (6:6), and if we have heard the enemy himself speak (6:4-5), then the time has now come in the present section for God to give Jeremiah metaphorical vineyard commands; and so he does (6:9). ("Gleaning," by the way, can imply destruction—cf. Judg. 20:45, with the same verb.) It is true that one verb here must be emended: *y*$^{e\text{c}}$*ôl*^{e}*lû* to *'ôlēl*, but the commentators all accept this emendation because of the following singular imperative *hāšēb* and the singular suffix of *yād*^{e}*kā*; the erroneous plural verb would be an understandable graphic slip, given the example of 5:10 and all the other plural imperatives. (Question: If in the fifth section we found 6:1 parallel to 4:5b-6, and 6:5 parallel to 4:7, is it totally fanciful to find here an assonantal parallel, *'ôlēl* plus *hāšēb* parallel to 4:8 *sipdû w*^{e}*hêlîlû*?)

Yahweh speaks in v. 9; Jeremiah answers in vv. 10-11a, and Yahweh speaks again in vv. 11b-15, so that here again we have the same threefold interchange that we found in the second and third sections.

This section is nicely linked to the one just preceding by the identical imperative that God offers both to the enemy and to Jeremiah: *šipkû*, "pour out (a siege-mound)," 6:6, and *š*^{e}*pōk*, "pour out (the wrath of Yahweh)," 6:11; note also the assonantal link of *sōl*^{e}*lâ*, "siege mound," in 6:6 with *salsillôt*, "tendrils," in 6:9.

There are also verbal reminiscences of earlier sections (we are approaching the close of the cycle, so that we expect to find recapitulations): with the first section (*šeber* 4:6, 6:14); with the second ("poor" and "great" 5:4-5, "small" and "great" 6:13); obviously with the third in the parallel of vineyard imagery, as well as in the calling of the prophet and the population listing by pairs (5:15-17, 6:11-12); and with the fourth (the reference to ears that do not hear—5:21, 6:10).

n. The Seventh Section: Again Orders that Turn Attention to Wisdom (6:16-26), and the Final Examination (6:27-30)

In my analysis of the identity of the speakers in the three battle scenes of the first section, I used 6:22-26 as an aid. Now that we have arrived at this last section, we see vv. 22-26 as the central subsection of three in the section: both the first (vv. 16-21) and the last (vv. 27-30) center on wisdom, and there is inclusio of *derek haṭṭôb* (v. 16) and *darkām* (v. 27) plus *ra'îm* (v. 29) and of *m's,* "reject" (6:19, 30). And if we have identified the speakers in vv. 22-26, we now ask who the speakers are in vv. 16-21 and vv. 27-30, for I suggest that there is symmetry here.

Let us begin with vv. 27-30. Earlier commentators saw no reason to assign any other speaker than Yahweh to the whole passage; more recent commentators have contrasted the speakers—in v. 27 Yahweh makes Jeremiah a tester, while in vv. 28-30 Jeremiah replies with his report (indeed, the third person "Yahweh" in v. 30 indicates as much).[50] I would agree.

But several considerations lead one to wonder whether Jeremiah is not also speaking in the last lines of vv. 16-17. (1) Something is wrong with vv. 16-17 as the words stand, if one assumes the speaker to be Yahweh all the way through the two verses—the second-person and third-person plurals alternate curiously; and the problem is only partly solved by the suggestion of Volz and Rudolph that a form of *'mr* first-person singular be inserted before the imperative "stand" in v. 16[51] to balance *wahᵃqimotî* at the beginning of v. 17. The disjunction would be solved by assuming a change of speaker. (2) The one earlier occurrence of *wayyo'mᵉrû* followed by a negative (5:12) is plainly in the mouth of Jeremiah;

this fact would not force us to make Jeremiah the speaker of the last lines of 6:16 and 17 (Yahweh could be "imitating" Jeremiah here!), but such evidence is suggestive, at least. It is perhaps significant that if one isolates all the quotations offered in the entire foe cycle proper (4:5-6:30), each quotation has a counterpart except 5:12: "Declare. . .proclaim" in 4:5 is repeated in 5:20; the pair in 4:10, 11 (*wā'ōmar*, "then I said," *yē'āmēr*, "it will be said" seem to be balanced by 5:2, 4 (*yō'meru*, "though they say," *wa'ᵃnî 'āmartî*, "then I said"); the pair in 4:29, 31 ("At the cry [*qôl*] 'Horseman and Archer,' " "For I heard the cry [*qôl*] of a woman. . .'woe is me' ") seem balanced by 6:4, 5 ("Prepare war against her," "Woe is us. . .," "Up and let us attack"). This balancing leaves 5:12 without any counterpart save the possibility of 6:16, 17, and does move us to take the possibility of a parallel seriously. (3) Beyond these considerations are others: I have already mentioned that the exchange in the last section (v. 27, Yahweh; vv. 28-30, Jeremiah) would suggest a similar exchange here; and certainly the quick exchange in 6:4-5 opens for us the possibility of a similar quick exchange here. All things considered, then, I propose Jeremiah as the speaker of the last lines of vv. 16 and 17. The rest of the material in vv. 16-21, of course, belongs in the mouth of Yahweh.

To sum up regarding the outline and identity of speakers in this section:

a. Orders that turn to wisdom (vv. 16-21)
   (i) v. 16a — Yahweh's battle orders that turn to wisdom
   (ii) v. 16b — Jeremiah's statement of the people's refusal
   (iii) v. 17a — Yahweh's statement of his sending watchmen in the past
   (iv) v. 17b — Jeremiah's statement of the people's refusal
   (v) vv. 18-21 — Yahweh's judgment on the people pronounced

b. Recapitulation: Once more the battle (vv. 22-26)
 (i) vv. 22-23 — Yahweh's description of the battle
 (ii) v. 24 — the people's expression of helplessness
 (iii) v. 25 — Yahweh's battle orders
 (iv) v. 26a — Jeremiah's last-ditch appeal to the people to repent
 (v) v. 26b — Jeremiah's hypothetical quotation of the people's lament

c. The Final Examination (vv. 27-30)
 (i) v. 27 — Yahweh's appointment of Jeremiah as his examiner
 (ii) vv. 28-30 — Jeremiah's report to Yahweh on the results of the examination.

Two new images are introduced in this section—"frankincense" and "sweet cane" in v. 20, and the assayer in vv. 27-30, which seem sudden and unexpected to the hearer unless he is alert to structural and assonantal phenomena. Let us take the frankincense and sweet cane first: they are the completion of a very lovely symmetry that goes back to 5:15. In 5:15 we are told that the foe is a nation from "far away and long ago": *mimmerḥaq, mēʿôlām*. In 6:16 Judah is told to search for the ancient paths, *nᵉtībôt ʿôlām*, where the good way is, *derek haṭṭôb*. Therefore we need a further use of *merḥaq* and *ṭôb*. Therefore, in 6:20 "sweet cane from a distant land," *qāneh haṭṭôb mēʾereṣ merḥāq*, and therefore its synonym, frankincense, from Sheba. Of such stuff is poetry made.

The "assayer" image also seems unexpected, but the bellows (*mappûaḥ*) in 6:29 echoes the pot blown (*nāpûaḥ*) in 1:13 (and indeed, is *sîr*, "pot," in 1:13 balanced by *sārê sôrᵉrîm* in 6:28?): the second vision in 1:13-14, we recall, referred directly to the foe from the north, and the unusual verb *pwḥ*[52] marks a kind of inclusio, the end of the foe cycle. However, there is another link between the assayer image and what has come before, and that is offered by the word *mbṣr* (v. 27). Vocalized as *mibṣār*, fortification (as in 4:5), it is plainly out of place, and since it is so vocalized in the MT, it has been treated by most commentators as a gloss.[53] But again, I think the consonants mark inclusio between 4:5 and the end here, and I think the word can be given an easy and plausible reading. In 6:9 Jeremiah was called to pass his hand again over the branches of the vineyard "like a grape-gatherer," *kᵉbôṣēr*. Here is the next "call" to Jeremiah, and is this not the word here? "I have made you an assayer rather than a grape-gatherer *(mibbôṣēr)* among my people." The preposition *min* has just this meaning elsewhere.[54] Incidentally, I see no reason to excise "bronze and iron" in v. 28 with several commentators; the passage shows good poetic structure, with an assonance of *nᵉḥōšet* with *bḥn* (v. 27) and *nāḥar mappûaḥ* (v. 29), and the discussion of 15:12 below (7, d) will offer further justification for retaining the phrase.

Now, if it is particularly the *first* subsection here (vv. 16-21) that reflects the *second* section (5:1-9) in the overall pattern of symmetry, and if the *second* subsection here (vv. 22-26) reflects the second battle scene in the first section (4:13-18),[55] then the *last* subsection here (vv. 27-30) helps to balance the otherwise unbalanced *fourth* section (Yahweh's monologue, 5:20-29); one notes that *bᵉʿammî* appears in the book of Jeremiah only in 5:26 and 6:27, and that *raʿ* appears in the foe cycle proper only in 5:28 (*rāʿ*) and 6:29 (*rāʿîm*). Indeed, one might almost detach 6:27-30 from the last section and call it a *coda.*

But when all is said and done, this section carries echoes of all the previous sections as well: the third *(merḥāq* and *ʿôlām);* the fourth, not only in the echoes in 6:27-30 but also, lightly, in the reference to the sea (6:23); the fifth insofar as the fifth echoes the first (references to "north" 6:1, 22; use of *sābîb* 6:3, 25); and with the sixth in the use of *yaḥdāw* in population listings (6:11, 12, 21) and in the double use of *kšl,* "stumble" (6:21), in parallel with the double use of its correlative *npl,* "fall" (6:15).

This completes the survey of the seven sections of the foe cycle proper, but before we draw any conclusions, let us take a closer look at the postlude in 8:4ff, which, according to the analysis already presented, is the true ending to the foe cycle.

o. A Closer Look at the Postlude (8:4-10a, 13)

We shall see in chapter 5 that the Temple Sermon and further prose (7:1-8:3) are intrusive here. Let us therefore turn to analyze the postlude. I have already indicated the linkage of 4:1-4 with 8:4ff (double *šwb* in 4:1 and 8:4) and of both 4:1-4 and 8:4ff to 5:2-3. I called 4:1-4 the *prelude*, and 8:4ff the *postlude*, but I have not yet defined the extent of the postlude with precision, nor analyzed its structure. The material between 8:4 and 13 offers several difficulties of text and interpretation, and we will do well to proceed with caution.

The material in vv. 8:4-5 offers several simultaneous parallels with earlier material; in reverse order of the earlier material we have: (1) "fall" and "rise" in v. 4, which echo the double "stumble" in 6:21 and the double "fall" in 6:15; (2) the phraseology of 8:5 that echoes 5:2 (already discussed);[56] (3) the double use of *šwb* in 8:4 that echoes the usage in the prelude, 4:1, and through it to the use of *šwb* in chapter 3 (already discussed);[57] and (4) the threefold question with *h*ᵃ-, *'im-*, *maddûaʿ*, which echoes that pattern in 2:14 and 2:31.

Let us now recall that the two occurrences in *h*ᵃ-, *'im-*, *maddûaʿ* in chapter 2 were keys to the structure there; they were prominent in the second and fourth subsections there and enclosed a third subsection whose key phrase was *'ēk tō'merî* (2:23).[58] Now we notice that just as *hă-, 'im-, maddûaʿ* introduce 8:4, so *'ēkâ tō'merû* introduces 8:8; vv. 4 and 8 begin the two respective subsections of the postlude—that is to say, the organization of the postlude is a reduced version of the organization of 2:5-37:

2:5-13 — (the first subsection)
2:14-19 — *hă-, 'im-, maddûaʿ* (v. 14) 8:4-7 — *hă-, 'im-, maddûaʿ* (v. 4)
2:20-25 — *'ēk tō'merî* (v. 23) 8:8ff — *'ēkâ tō'merû* (v. 8)
2:26-37 — *hă-, 'im-, maddûaʿ* (v. 31).

(One may note in passing that 8:8 may have been stimulated by Isa. 19:11, "How can you say. . .'I am a son of the wise'?")[59]

Structurally speaking, therefore, 8:4-8 manages to make a link with the last two sections of the foe cycle ("fall"), with the second section ("they hold fast to deceit, they refuse to return"), to the prelude and therefore to chapter 3 (double *šwb*), and to the structure of chapter 2.

Now, if 8:8 begins the second half of the postlude, how far does it continue? These verses are heavy with echoes of earlier material. I have already dealt with "how can you say" at the beginning of v. 8. The phrase "we are wise," *ḥăkāmîm 'ănaḥnû*, echoes *ḥăkāmîm hēmmâ lehāraʿ* in 4:22 (thus the first section of the foe cycle).[60] The phrase *'āken. . .laššeqer* in 8:8 picks up *lākēn* (read with 20 MSS *'ākēn*) *laššeqer* in 5:2 (again 5:2-3!). The phrase *tôrat-yhwh* in 8:8 picks up *tôrātî* (*i.e.,* of Yahweh) in 6:19, and "fields and wives to others" in 8:10a echoes 6:12. Now 8:10b-12 is not original here, but a secondary doublet triggered by 8:10a, which is very like 6:12; Weiser is surely correct in his contention that v. 13 is the original ending of v. 10a. Verse 13 offers textual difficulties that may never be solved with confidence, but we can at least sense the structure here, and notice that v. 13 offers a parallel to 6:9 (*gepen* with synonyms for "gather").

I see no reason to link v. 13 with vv. 14ff[61]—the repetition of *'sp* is a verbal link with the next cycle, for 8:14 replicates diction from 4:5, and we are off into something new. The postlude, then, breaks into two halves—8:4-7, and 8:8-10a, 13, and rounds off not only the foe cycle but the harlotry cycle as well.

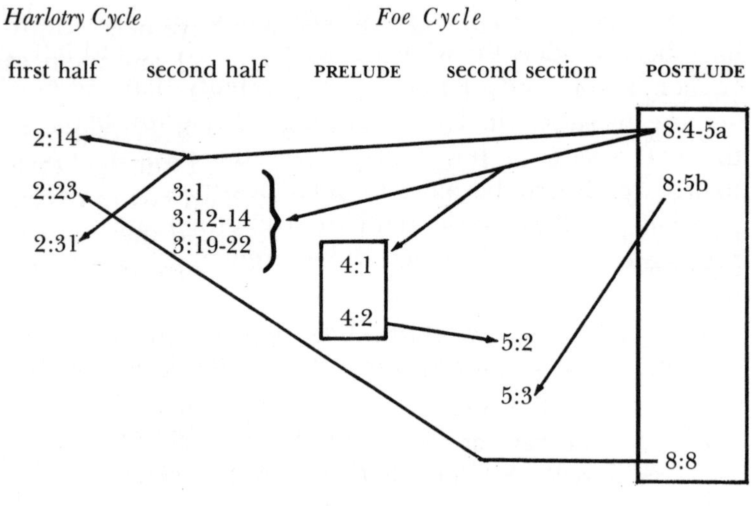

p. Conclusions, and Some Perspective: Parallels in Earlier Prophetic Material?

I shall discuss the overall conclusions in detail when I have completed the analysis of chapters 1-20, but let me offer here some provisional conclusions. For if the foregoing analysis has substance, it raises some very basic issues in my assessment of the material in the early chapters of the book of Jeremiah.

First, the identication of the speakers in these passages must call into question any commentary material that does not identify the speaker by sound use of data. Obviously the exegesis of a passage must begin with the identification of the speaker. In particular, I must underscore what I feel to be the error of any theory of a "blending" of voices.

Second, the discovery of the unified cycles of material of the scope found in chapters 2-3 and 4-6 is a surprise. The question immediately arises as to whether there are not patterns in earlier prophetic material that could have been models for what we seem to have found here. Earlier in the study I noted the possibility that the earlier use of *maqqēl* in Hos. 4:12 might be a link between the first vision in Jer. 1:11-12 and the harlotry cycle, hence we should be alert to such possibilities. Finding possible parallels would tend to strengthen the case of the existence of such structure in Jeremiah; it would not then be a question of *creatio ex nihilo.*

There is a sharp break in Hosea between 5:7 and 5:8; indeed, Edwin Good sees this break as the basic division between 4:4 and 14:1.[62] The material in 4:4-5:7 is dominated by the themes of knowledge and harlotry;[63] 5:8 begins with a line similar to those in Jer. 4:5 and 6:1:

Hos. 5:8 *tiqʻû šôp̄ār baggibʻâ*
Jer. 4:5 *tiqʻû šôpar baʼareṣ*
Jer. 6:1 *ûbitqôaʻ tiqʻû šôpār.*

There is no other imperative of this verb in any other relevant prophetic material.[64] I suggest, then, that this pattern of "harlotry" plus "sound the trumpet" in Hosea stimulated the sequence in Jeremiah.[65]

The first five chapters of Isaiah offer another kind of possible parallel. Analysis of the way the material in those chapters were collected are many and various, but one defensible scheme would certainly center around the word "vineyard". It is surely significant that Isa. 1:8 has *bat,* "daughter," and *kerem,* while 5:10 has *kerem* and *bat* (a measure). In any event, prominent between these two points are other passages in which *kerem* is used —concretely in 3:14, and, more important, metaphorically in the famous "song of the vineyard" (5:1-7), where it appears six times to refer to Israel. Whether this "vineyard" scheme points to the original structure of Isa. 1-5 or not, it is certainly prominent enough to have commended itself to Jeremiah: the alternation of metaphorical use and concrete use, which we find in the foe cycle of Jeremiah (5:10, 6:9; 5:17), and the association of *'kl* with "daughter(s)" (Isa. 1:7-8), which we find in the foe cycle of Jeremiah (5:17).

Indeed, one might be tempted to see the parallel of "sound the trumpet" and "raise a signal" in Jer. 4:5-6 as a sharing of the stimuli from Hosea ("sound the trumpet," Hos. 5:8) and Isaiah ("he will raise a signal," Isa. 5:26—for the material in Isa. 5:26-30 resembles greatly the description of the foe from the north in Jeremiah). One notes also the coincidence of Hos. 5:9 (*l^ešammâ tiḫyeh*) and Isa. 5:9 (*l^ešammâ yihyû*),[66] and the fact that *mē'ên yôšēb,* Isa. 5:9, is repeated in Jer. 4:7.[67] It looks as if the contrast between harlotry and war in Hos. 4:4-5:7 and 5:8ff, and the vineyard imagery of Isa. 1-5, and phraseology from both corpora, found their place in helping to shape the structure of the material in Jer. 2-6.[68]

5

The Temple Sermon and Further Prose (7:1-8:3)

BEFORE examining the "supplementary foe cycle" (8:14ff), let us pause to take account of the Temple Sermon and further prose in 7:1-8:3. This passage, as we shall see in a moment, was added at a later stage in the growth of the corpus of Jeremianic material. The task here is twofold—to discern the inner structure of this passage, and to establish why it was inserted at this point.

Commentators have differed both as to how much of this prose material reflects what was actually delivered in the Temple court, and as to how to "outline" the passage. From the point of view of the analysis offered here, there is no reason why we cannot see the end of the Temple Sermon proper at v. 15, v. 19, or v. 20. This will become clear in the details that follow.

The passage, as presently constituted, is held together

by the word *māqôm* (7:3, 6,[1] 7, 12, 14, 20, 32, 8:3).[2] This word has appeared previously in the book of Jeremiah only at 4:7, and that occurrence seems irrelevant to the placement of this passage. But 7:2 begins with *ʿ*a*mōd*, while 6:16, the beginning of the last subdivision of the foe cycle, began with *ʿimdû*;[3] this association may be one reason for the placement of 7:1ff here.

Structurally, the material through v. 19 is bound together by nominative and accusative pronouns: *hēmmâ* (v. 4) as the central item in vv. 3-7; *ʾattem* (v. 8) at the head of vv. 8-15; *w*e*ʾattâ* and *ʾōtak* (v. 16) at the head of vv. 16-19; *hēmmâ* in v. 17; *hēm* sandwiched between *haʾōtî* and *h*a*lōʾ ʾōtām* in v. 19. Again, we cannot be sure whether vv. 16ff were understood to have been spoken at the time vv. 3-15 were, or whether vv. 16-19 are simply present here because of association of ideas and pronouns; nevertheless, in their present position they offer a unity.

In the meantime there are other structural features of vv. 3-19: vv. 3-7 have an obvious unity in themselves, v. 3 paralleling vv. 5-7, leaving v. 4 the middle term that receives the spotlight. Verses 8-15 are linked with vv. 3-7 by *māqôm* twice (vv. 3, 7; 12, 14), by "you are trusting in the words of the lie" (vv. 4, 8),[4] and by the thematic link between Shiloh and Jerusalem. Verses 16-19 give related material regarding Jeremiah's function; there is the parallelism of "hear" and "see" (vv. 16, 17).

Verse 20 looks as if it were an addendum, a *māqôm*-saying added here because of the root *bʿr* (qal, "burn," v. 20; hiphil, "kindle," v. 17). It certainly does not participate in the structure of pronouns of vv. 3-19, and it carries a fresh introduction, *lākēn kōh ʾāmar ʾ*a*dōnāy yhwh.*[5]

Verses 21-34 offer something else: a nice parallelism

to two verses toward the end of the foe cycle—6:20-21. In this regard, the previous material in chapter 7 has paved the way—we have already seen a possible parallel between 7:2, *ʿ*ᵃ*mōd*, and 6:16, *ʿimdû*; but the parallels continue: *r'h* 6:16, and *šmʿ* 6:18, parallel to *šmʿ* 7:16, *r'h* 7:17; possibly *p*ᵉ*rî* 6:19, 7:20. But these are commonplace words and are not particularly noteworthy. To see the operative parallels with 6:20-21, we should first note that 7:21-34 breaks into three parts: vv. 21-26, where the theme-word is *'ābôt,* "fathers" (vv. 22, 25, 26); vv. 27-29, a unit that turns once more to Jeremiah's function, and offers one or two scraps of poetry; and vv. 30-34, where the theme-word is *bānîm* (and related forms), "children/sons," (vv. 30, v. 31 three times: "son," "sons," "daughters," v. 32, and perhaps reinforced by the bridegroom-bride pairing in v. 34)—and also should note the assonance with *bānû* in v. 31. This series of units, we remind ourselves, contains *māqôm* as well (v. 32). Now the linking of "fathers" and "sons" is anticipated in the previous unit (7:18), but it is evidently the pairing in 6:21 that is operative here, perhaps reinforced by "daughter" twice, vv. 23, 26. For we have in the previous verse in chapter 6 the pairing *ʿōlôtêkem, zibḥêkem;* and these are the theme-words paired twice in the head of this first subsection, 7:21, 22. We may note further that the two verbs in 6:21 are *kšl* and *'bd;* it is surely no coincidence that *'bd* is found in the first scrap of poetry, 7:28, and the assonantal *šlk* in 7:29!

One must hasten to add that other things may be afoot here; one has the impression that the whole of chapter 7 is a kind of midrash on Deut. 12:1-7 (note the parallels: *māqôm,* Deut. 12:2, 5;[6] Yahweh's name, Deut. 12:5, Jer. 7:12; "your burnt offerings and your sacrifices," Deut. 12:6, Jer. 7:21; "eat," Deut. 12:7, Jer.

7:21; *śmḥ* Deut. 12:7, Jer. 7:34). But in its immediate context Jer. 7 looks like a parallel in thematic words to 6:16-21.

I would take 8:1-3 as an appendix.[7] It is in a slightly different style ("bones," five times; *wa'ᵃšer* five times) and would seem to be here only because it likewise has *māqôm,* and because it comments on 7:33. (Question: is "be gathered," 8:1, stimulated by "gather" in 8:13, 14?)

In sum, chapter 7 was inserted here because of verbal associations with 6:16ff; it offers a series of related prose units united by *māqôm,* as follows:

a. Temple Sermon proper?—7:3-15: *hēmmâ, 'attem*
b. Jeremiah's role: do not intercede — 7:16-19: *'attâ, hēm*
c. An insertion on God's destruction — 7:20
d. A trio of passages on false worship (7:21-34):
  (i) regarding the fathers — vv. 21-26
  (ii) miscellany on Jeremiah's role — vv. 27-29
  (iii) regarding the children — vv. 30-34
e. An appendix, with commentary on v. 33 — 8:1-3.

6
The Supplementary Foe Cycle and Related Material (8:14-10:25)

a. The Sections of the Supplementary Foe Cycle; Phraseological Parallels to the First Foe Cycle

Verse 8:14 mimics 4:5, but now the walled cities are no longer a refuge; they have become traps for the victims within. Things have become much worse. The material that follows continues to ring the changes on the foe cycle: again there are battle scenes (8:16); again Jeremiah is overcome with dismay (8:18), again there are appeals to wisdom (9:2), again the people will be refined and tested (9:6). The phraseological parallels between the two poetic collections are cumulatively impressive and will be detailed below. But first we need to define the extent of the collection, which begins in 8:14.

Since the material deals again with the foe from the

north, we look again for imperatives and again we are rewarded:

8:14 — *hēʼāsᵉpû*
9:16 — *hitbônᵉnû ûqirʼû ûtᵉbôʼênâ šilḥû*
9:19 — *šᵉmaʻnâ wᵉlammēdnâ*
10:17 — *ʼispî.*

In addition, there is a cohortative in 9:14, and jussives in 9:17 and 19. (There are two additional imperatives: 10:24, *yassᵉrēnî*, and 10:25, *šᵉpōk*, but they are addressed to Yahweh, and are not therefore relevant, strictly speaking. Further, the LXX and Peshitta read *ʼeśśāʼ* in 9:9 not as an imperfect but as an imperative (thus *śᵉʼû*), probably correctly. But this verb is second in its colon rather than first, so that again it is not quite analogous to the others. Later we shall see that 9:9 is the beginning of a short "interlude.")

The imperatives before us lay out, then, a cycle of three sections, beginning with 8:14, 9:16, and 10:17 respectively. The second section obviously ends at 9:21; I shall leave open for the moment the extent of the first and third sections. Question: in the first foe cycle, multiple imperatives were to be found in the first, the balancing fifth, and the last sections, while the second, third, and fourth sections had one imperative apiece. (The sixth had two.) Do we have the opposite (but still symmetrical) pattern here?—namely, that the first and last sections offer one imperative apiece, while the middle one offers multiple imperatives? It would seem so. At any rate, the first and last sections here offer battle scenes, while the middle one has quite another content, so that we have an A-B-A' form.

The parallels in phraseology between this "supplementary foe cycle" and the first foe cycle begin in 8:14 and continue through 9:7;[1] are found in 9:19, 20, and again in 10:19-21. So again we find ourselves with three sections. Let me list these parallels now in detail, in the order in which they appear in the present supplementary foe cycle, together with notes on their frequency or infrequency of occurrence elsewhere.

1. *hē'āsᵉpû wᵉnābô'(â) 'el 'ārê hammibṣār*	8:14	4:5	no other //s in Jer.
2. *qôl* linked with "Dan"	8:16	4:15	"Dan" not otherwise in Jer.
3. horses (of the enemy) plus a ref. to a city (4:13 Jerus., 6:23 Zion, 8:16 "city")	8:16	4:13 6:23	other refs. to "horses" in Jer. are not in contexts of destruction
4. *r'š*, "quake"	8:16	4:24	otherwise in Jer.: 10:10 (idols), 49:21, 51:29
5. *yš'* niphal, "be saved"	8:20	4:14	otherwise in Jer.: Jer. to Yahweh 17:14; eschatological promise 23:6, 33:16; 30:7 (ironic?)
6. *šeber* plus *'ammî*	8:21	6:14	8:11 is a doublet; this combination not otherwise in Jer.
7. (high emotion) has seized (*ḥzq* hiphil) us/me: 6:24 *ṣārâ* plus *-nû*; 8:21 *šammâ* plus *-nî*	8:21	6:24	otherwise in Jer.: 49:24, 50:43
8. *n'p*, "commit adultery"	9:1	5:7	otherwise in Jer.: 13:27 (noun), 23:10, 14; 3:7-11 (midrash); 7:9 (Temple Sermon); 29:23 (letter to the Exiles)
9. *bgd*, "deal treacherously"	9:1	5:11	otherwise in Jer.: 3:20, 12:1, 6
10. *lō' le'ᵉmûnâ*	9:2	5:2	not otherwise in Jer.

11. *'ōtî lō' yādā'û*	9:2	4:22	not otherwise in Jer. (even in nonpausal form)
12. *rākîl*, "slanderer"	9:3	6:28	not otherwise in Jer.
13. *mirmâ*, "treachery"	9:5, 7	5:27	not otherwise in Jer.
14. *bḥn* and *ṣrp*, "refine"	9:6	6:27, 29	*ṣrp* not otherwise in Jer.
15. women making mourning (in a variety of vocabulary)	9:19	6:26	no other passages in Jer.
16. *'ôlāl* parallel to *baḥûrîm*, plus *ḥûṣ*	9:20	6:11	not otherwise in Jer.
17. *'armᵉnôt*, "palaces"	9:20	6:5	otherwise in Jer.: to be rebuilt 30:18; pal. of Jerus. 17:27; pal. of Damascus 49:27
18. *makkâ*, "wound," plus *ḥᵒlî*, "sickness"	10:19	6:7	not otherwise in Jer.
19. *'ōhel*, "tent," parallel to *yᵉrî'ôt*, "curtains," with *šdd* pual followed by an expression for "*stupid*" (4:22 *sākāl*, 10:21 *b'r*)	10:20f	4:20, 22	not otherwise in Jer.

One may also add the formula X-preposition-X, where "X" stands for a given noun; I have noted 4:20, *šeber 'al-šeber*, and the following at the beginning of chapter 9: *mērā'â 'el-rā'â*, v. 2; *mirmâ bᵉmirmâ*, v. 5 (and the preceding *tōk bᵉtôk*, if the reconstruction of the text usually suggested is correct). Obviously, it is difficult to devise a way to locate any other passages that contain this formula, but I am not aware of other occurrences.

There may well be other items that I have not discovered, to add to such a list, but even so this list is cumulatively impressive. These passages are not doublets. The material in chapters 8-10 offer these words and phrases in quite fresh poetic contexts.

I began the discussion of the supplementary foe cycle by remarking that in 8:14 the fortified cities no longer afford the protection they did in 4:5; and in these other parallel items also, one has the impression that there is a growing seriousness to the people's plight, that things are growing worse. Thus #5: in comparing 4:14 and 8:20 one has the feeling that 8:20 really refers to the "eleventh hour." And #14: Jeremiah is the assayer in 6:27-30, while Yahweh himself has taken over the task in 9:6.

Now that the form of the cycle is tolerably clear, we may examine the sections one by one, grappling with the problem that engaged us in the first foe cycle—the identification of speakers.

b. The First Section: Battle Scenes and Wisdom Concerns (8:14-9:8)

In 4:5 Yahweh spoke and told the people what to say. In 8:14 the people say it: "Gather together, let us go into the fortified cities." So 8:14 is more than an echo of 4:5; with the sarcastic addition "and perish there," it is a kind of *response* to God's command in 4:5. Obviously, then, in vv. 14-15 the people speak. In v. 17, just as obviously, Yahweh speaks, and I would suggest that he is also the speaker in v. 16, both because the diction and phraseology imitate the speeches of Yahweh in the first foe cycle (*e.g.*, 4:7, 15) and because the structure of vv. 16-17 parallels the structure of vv. 14-15 (v. 14, *yōšᵉbîm*, *ʿārê*; v. 16, *ʿîr, yōšᵉbê*; vv. 15 and 17, *ʾên*).

In 8:18 we have diction and phraseology that remind us of 4:19ff. While there is no proof that these lines could not be a speech of Yahweh's, it seems plain that we should follow the lead of 4:19ff (and the consequent opinion of commentators) and assign this passage to Jeremiah. The prophet quotes the lament of the people in the second half of v. 19a; Yahweh interrupts in v. 19b.[2] The people finish lamely in v. 20, and Jeremiah himself in v. 21. We have here, then, the kind of quick conversational interchange we found in 6:4-5 and 6:16-17. Verses 22-23 offer a parallel mood to the material in vv. 18-21 and are likewise spoken by Jeremiah; vv. 18-21 and 22-23 are linked by the threefold-question pattern *hᵃ-, 'im-, maddûᵃ'* (vv. 18, 22) and by the fourfold use of *bat-'ammi* in two inclusiones (vv. 19, 21, 22, 23). The double use of the triple question of course helps to link this opening section of the present cycle to the postlude of the first cycle (8:4). But if v. 22 uses the triple-question pattern, v. 23 plunges ahead into new phraseology (which, however, marvelously mimics a phrase in v. 14: v. 23 *rō'šî mayim,* "my head (to be) water," v. 14 *mê-rō'š,* "water of poison").

I would suggest, however (against all the commentators), that 9:1-2 is a speech in the mouth of Yahweh. In 4:22 we had Yahweh's answer to 4:19-21, with the suggestion of word-play there *(mē'ay-'ammî);* here, I submit, we have a similar situation: parallel word-usage *(mî yittēn)* with contrasting mood (bitterness in 9:1-2 in contrast with frustrated compassion in 8:22-23). But there are more clues. The only other relevant occurrence of the root *lyn,* "lodge for the night," in the book of Jeremiah is 14:8,[3] and in 14:8 the subject is Yahweh. Furthermore, 9:2 carries the phrase *'ōtî lō' yādā'û,* the phrase that appeared in Yahweh's speech in 4:22. (And, as I have already noted in the listing of this parallel (above, #11), there are no other parallels to this precise phrase elsewhere in Jeremiah.) Commentators have seen the problem of the personal reference in this phrase, and so Volz, Rudolph, and Bright propose to emend *'ōtî* to *'et-yhwh* (because, as Rudolph noted in the critical apparatus of Kittel's *Biblia Hebraica* (3rd ed.), "propheta loquitur"!)—an emendation that I suggest is wrong. If this proposal is sound, then it opens up the possibility of a far more acute understanding of Jeremiah's perception of the tension between himself and Yahweh in their respective attitudes toward the people.[4]

Verses 3-5 offer a fresh passage, also spoken by Yahweh: the pun on "Jacob," and then more material using "tongue" and "lie," ending with two twin-noun phrases ("oppression on oppression," "deceit on deceit"—if the MT is emended in the way most commentators do) that echo "evil to evil" in v. 2. Note that Volz, Rudolph, and Bright again emend *'ōtî* in v. 5 to *'et-yhwh,* under the assumption that Jeremiah is speaking; this is not called for.

Verses 6-8 are again spoken by Yahweh; it is hard to know whether we have here a third subsection of a triplet made up of vv. 1-2, 3-5, and 6-8, or whether vv. 6-8 should not rather be considered a separate conclusion to the whole section. I shall take the latter course, since it is a kind of reprise of the whole section; it not only picks up the imagery of the "tongue," "arrow," and "slander" of vv. 2-4, but the mention of "peace" in v. 7 echoes 8:15, and there are even wider echoes: *rākîl*, "slanderer," in 9:3 triggers the use of the "testing/refining" image in v. 6 because of the association of these words in 6:28, and the refrain in 9:8 is identical with that in 5:9 and 29 (that is to say, this section ends with a refrain identical with that by which the second and fourth sections of the first foe cycle ended).

To sum up, then:

a. The first interchange (8:14-17)
   (i) the people's acknowledgement of the battle emergency, vv. 14-15
   (ii) Yahweh's description of more battle horrors, vv. 16-17
b. Two double speeches of Jeremiah and Yahweh (8:18-9:5)
   (i) Jeremiah:
      —quotes the people, is interrupted by Yahweh, vv. 18-21
      hᵃ-, 'im-, maddûᵃ', v. 18
      —wishes his eyes were tears, vv. 22-23
      hᵃ-, 'im-, maddûᵃ', v. 22.
   (ii) Yahweh:
      —wishes he could go to the desert, 9:1-2
      "evil to evil," v. 2
      —offers a word-play on "Jacob," vv. 3-5
      "oppression on oppression," "deceit on deceit," v. 5
c. Yahweh's conclusion (9:6-8).

I have already implied the parallels between this section and various sections of the first foe cycle: its parallel to the first section there in the presentation of the battle and Jeremiah's emotional reaction to it, and of Yahweh the schoolmaster answering with his own set of norms; to the second and fourth sections there in similar wisdom motifs, and the use of the refrain of 5:9 and 29; and to the last section (in its "coda") in the reference to refining. One might also say that there is stress on the heart *(leb)* in the first cycle, and on the tongue here.

c. The Interlude (9:9-10)

These two verses are curious. Negatively, one may say, first of all, that they are not part of the first section; that section clearly ends with v. 8, with its refrain identical with that in 5:9, 29. Second, they are not part of the second section, which just as clearly begins in v. 16 with its feminine references. Third, they do not make up a separate section: the first verb, even if read as an imperative (with LXX and Peshitta), does not come first in its colon as imperatives elsewhere in the cycle do, and the two verses are hardly substantial enough to merit the designation *section.* Fourth, the verses give no evidence of being a secondary insertion here: there are no obvious catchword links with what has come before. (The link between "weeping," *b^{e}kî*, parallel with *w^{e}'ebkeh*, 8:23, has another explanation, as I shall now show.)

Positively, these two verses offer three kinds of links: (1) with each of the three sections of this supplementary foe cycle; (2) with the opening section of the first foe cycle; and (3) with the first half of the harlotry cycle. This is a large accomplishment for two verses!

Specifically: the phrase "weeping and wailing," *b^{e}kî wanehî,* in v. 9, links the verses to both the first section, with *w^{e}'ebkeh*, 8:23, and to the second section, where *n^{e}hî/nehî* occurs three times, 9:17, 18, 19. (Note that no form of *n^{e}hi* occurs in the first section[5] and no form of *bkh* occurs in the second section.[6]) The link with the second section is reinforced by *qînâ,* 9:9, 19. The link with the third section is "lair of jackals," *m^{e}'ôn tannîm*, which occurs only in 9:10 and 10:22, and nowhere else in the first twenty chapters.[7]

As to links with the first foe cycle and with the harlotry cycle, if we attempt in these two verses to find parallels to the material in the first foe cycle as we did for 8:14-9:8, 9:16-21, and 10:17-25,[8] we find them, true enough—two parallels, to be exact—but we also find intermixed with them three parallels to chapter 2, that is, to the first half of the harlotry cycle, a phenomenon that we do not find to any significant degree in the rest of this supplementary foe cycle.

1. *niṣṣᵉtû mibbᵉlî*	9:9	2:15	*yṣt* niphal not otherwise in Jer.
2. negative with *'br* qal plus *'îš*	9:9	2:6	not otherwise in Jer.
3. *'ôp* plus *nāḏᵉdû/nāḏāḏû*	9:9	4:25	not otherwise in Jer.
4. *šammâ/šᵉmāmâ* plus *mibbelî/me'ên yôšēb*	9:10	2:15, 4:7	this combination not otherwise in Jer.

When I came upon earlier material that shared parallels with both the foe cycle and the harlotry cycle, I called them the prelude and the postlude to the first foe cycle. This present brief passage, then, I must call the *interlude,* and it seems to carry on the same function: to bind together earlier material to what is at the moment being presented. Let us compare the diagram of the prelude and postlude (4, o, and below) with an analogous diagram we can construct for the interlude (see next page):

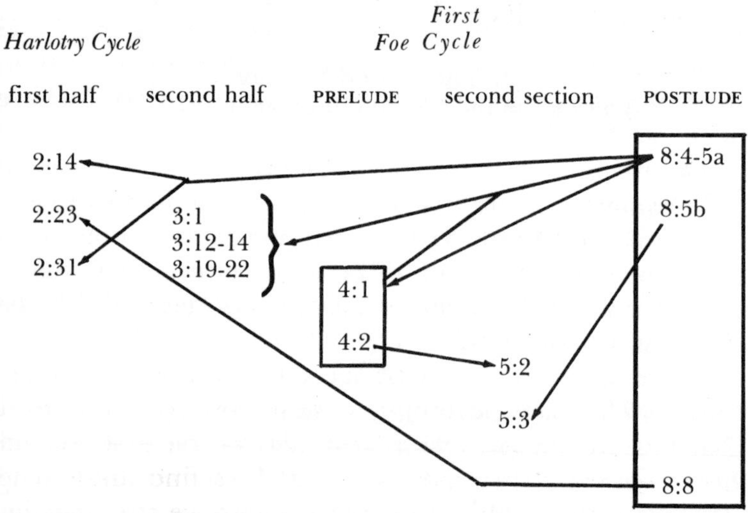

These diagrams suggest that the interlude helps to turn the structure of this supplementary foe cycle "inside out," so to speak, in comparison with that of the first foe

Harlotry Cycle *First Foe Cycle* *Supplementary Foe Cycle*

first half | first section | first section | INTERLUDE | second section | third section

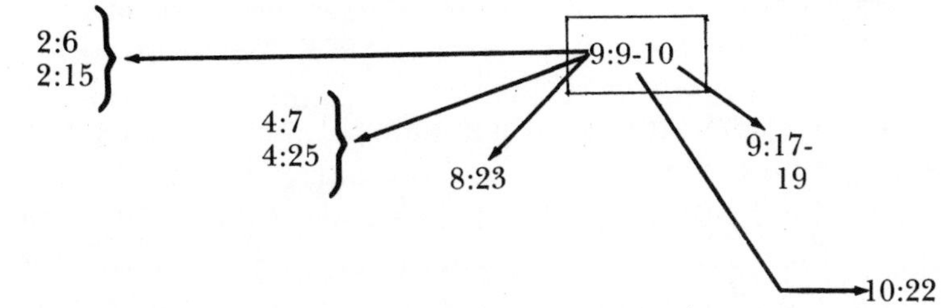

cycle, in just the same way that the symmetry of the single-imperative/multiple-imperative occurrences have been reversed (see above, 6,a).

Yahweh is evidently speaking (v. 10), as he did in the prelude and postlude of the first cycle.

d. The Second Section: The Call to the Women to Lament (9:16-21)

This section is short and straightforward and needs little comment. Here is something new: imperatives that are feminine plural. The people speak the whole passage (the first phrase of v. 21 is of course unoriginal), and in a way this section echoes the concerns of 4:8, as the first section of this cycle began by an imitation of 4:5. There are two subsections here (namely, vv. 16-18 and 19-21), each beginning with imperatives. We note that this section ends with *’sp* (v. 21) as the first section began with it (8:14); indeed, it may be significant that v. 21 ends with *’ên* plus *’sp* as the postlude of the first foe cycle ends with double *’sp* and double *’ên* (8:13).[9] It may also be that the verb "teach" (*lmd* piel) in v. 19 echoes its earlier occurrence in the first section, 9:4.

e. The Third Section:
Once More, Battle Scenes (10:17-25)

As the first section began with *'sp,* and the second section ended with the same verb, so this third one begins with it once more; but whereas 8:14 (and its parent 4:5) had *hammibṣār* "(cities of) fortification," this verse has *bammāṣôr,* "under seige." The situation is growing wilder!

One senses some kind of pun on "Canaan" in v. 17. Is this parallel to the pun on "Jacob" toward the end of the first section? and indeed, are not both these puns parallels to the puns on "Jacob" and "Canaan" respectively in Hos. 12:3-4, 8? It would seem a likely possibility.[10]

Verse 18 is clearly spoken by Yahweh, and one assumes the same for v. 17; Yahweh was the speaker of the "Jacob" pun in 9:3.

With verses 19-21 we have the problem of identifying the speakers once more. There are many factors to be considered here. In diction this passage is closely reminiscent of 4:19-22 (*šeber* 4:20, *šibrî* 10:19; "my tents are destroyed" 4:20, "my tent is destroyed" 10:20; "my curtains" 4:20, 10:20; the theme of stupidity, with different vocabulary, in 4:22 and 10:21). However, in 10:21 Yahweh is referred to in the third person, in contrast to the first-person references in 4:22, and this circumstance suggests that the speaker in 10:21 is not Yahweh, as was the case in 4:22. This assumption suggests, by symmetry, that the speaker in 10:19-20 is not Jeremiah, as was the case in 4:19-21. The next problem is whether *wa'anî 'āmartî 'ak. . .*in 10:19b marks a change of speaker; we note that the previous occurrence of this phrase (5:4) did *not* mark such a change. If the analogy holds, then we are led to assume one speaker, other than Jeremiah, for all of 10:19-20. Given the evident echo in v. 19, *'ôy-lî,* of 4:31, *'ôy-nā' lî,*[11] where the people spoke, and given the parallel occurrences of *makkâ* and *hᵒlî* in 6:7 in the mouth of the people, and the reference to "my children" in 10:20—more likely in the mouth of the people than of Jeremiah, we have the following: 10:19-20—the people; 10:21—Jeremiah.

Verse 22 is a reprise, describing the battle once more. We have become accustomed to assigning these to Yahweh, and there is no reason why this assignment is not correct here.

Now what we are to make of 10:23-24 and 25? Verses 23-24 have received the most varied treatment. The personal references in the text have been read variously: Voltz emends "I know" (v. 23) to "thou knowest"; and most commentators accept the LXX readings in v. 24 ("us," twice) instead of the MT ("me").[12] Some take the words as a prayer by Jeremiah on behalf of the people (Cornill, Weiser, Bright), or as a "confession" like 11:18ff—a prayer for himself (Hyatt); others take the words as uttered by the people for themselves (Volz, Condamin). Some even doubt its authenticity (Volz).

Condamin is right; this is a prayer of the people for themselves. But Volz is wrong; the verses are genuine to Jeremiah. The MT, furthermore, is correct: *yāda'tî* in v. 23 is parallel with *'āmartî* in v. 19b, and the *-nî* suffixes in v. 24 are parallel with *'ôy lî* in v. 19a. The singular is corporate.[13] The point that has been missed in the commentaries, however, is that this is Jeremiah's final "stinger." The people speak in v. 23, by quoting Prov. 16:9—the likeness of wording is very close.[14] The people feel justified in affirming irresponsibility ("I know, Yahweh, that a man does not have his way of life within his own power") by quoting scripture, much as king Ahaz quoted scripture to justify his not putting Yahweh to the test (Isa. 7:12). They then ask Yahweh, if he is to punish them at all, to do so modestly and gently—and as Jeremiah frames the prayer, it is the height of fatuity and irony. The people have not gotten the point, any more than they had in 8:19-20, an earlier fatuous utterance of the people. They are responding to the constant pleas of Yahweh to look to the right *derek* (6:16) by abdicating their responsibility. The Jerusalem Bible has the singular pronouns plural, but it has caught the tone of irresponsibility perfectly:

> Well you know, Yahweh,
> the course of man is not in his control,
> nor is it in man's power as he goes his way
> to guide his steps.
> Correct us [MT me], Yahweh, gently,
> not in your anger or you will reduce us [MT me]
> to nothing.

The fear expressed at the end of v. 24, of course, is that Yahweh will overturn the promise made to the patriarchs to make of the nation a *gôy gādôl*. Since the *māgôr-missābîb* episode (20:1-6) seems to demonstrate the same preoccupation of Jeremiah's part, it is not surprising to find it here.[15]

Verse 25 is universally rejected as nongenuine: it quotes with only minor variation Psalm 79:6-7. But suppose Jeremiah has the people here quote this nationalistic verse as a perfect vehicle for their nationalistic notions—what then? Would this not be a crashing climax to the last section of the cycle? We note that the poetic structure of v. 25 is well integrated into what has preceded: the singular imperative *šᵉpōk*, addressed to Yahweh, is an ironic reversal of the same imperative, with the same object, addressed to Jeremiah in 6:11: in 6:11 Yahweh tells Jeremiah to pour out the divine wrath on the various sections of Judah; in 10:25 the people tell Yahweh to pour out his divine wrath on the nations. Further, *ḥᵃmatᵉkā* in v. 25 in parallel to *'appᵉkā* in v. 24; *mišpᵉḥôt* in v. 25 is in assonance with *mišpāṭ* in v. 24; the verb *'kl* in v. 25 recalls the repetitions of that verb in 5:17. If we did not know of Psalm 79:6-7, we would accept this verse as the climax of the oracle. Why may it not be all the more a climax now that we know it to be a citation (just as v. 23 was a citation)?

But there is a further possibility. We recall that the prelude to the first foe cycle, 4:1-4, carried quotations —the reminiscence of the promises of Yahweh to Abraham in Genesis, in Jer. 4:2b, and the virtual quotations from Hosea and Deuteronomy in 4:3-4.[16] Now, here in 10:24 we have a plea that Yahweh not overturn the promises to Abraham, followed in v. 25 by a quotation from a nationalistic psalm. It looks very much as if we have here an inclusio *by quotation*.[17] It looks very much as if Jeremiah is saying here, by implication: God had hoped in times past to fulfill his promise given to Abraham in Genesis, but the only way that promise could be fulfilled is by your heeding the word he gave to you in Hosea and Deuteronomy. Since, instead, you persist in heeding only Psalm 79, he has no choice but to overturn the promise to Abraham.

I may repeat once more the tentative suggestion I made when we were analyzing Jer. 4:3-4,[18] that 4:3-4 may have been *inserted* at that point as an inclusio to 10:23-25 *at the time when* the supplementary foe cycle was added to the first foe cycle. The suggestion is not necessary, of course, to the analysis here, but it is at least a possibility.

Finally, we may note that *yāda'tî* in v. 23 echoes *yᵉda'tîkā* in 1:5; here is an inclusio that carries us all the way back to the call.[19] I suggest, in sum, that v. 25 ends the supplementary foe cycle.

But there is one more possibility: that the supplementary foe cycle originally ended at 10:22 (with the final reprise of a battle scene, reminiscent thus of 4:5-7), and that 10:23-25 (and 4:3-4?) were added at the time the confessional collection (found within chapters 11-20) was added to the corpus.[20] It would be best to call 10:23-25 a "coda," and leave open the question of when it became part of the supplementary foe cycle.

The outline of the last section would then be:

a. Yahweh's description of the battle scene (vv. 17-18)
b. A dialogue between the people and Jeremiah:
   (i) the people lament their fate (vv. 19-20)
   (ii) Jeremiah speaks of the stupidity of the leaders (v. 21)
c. Yahweh's final description of the battle scene (v. 22)
d. A coda: the people demonstrate their incapacity to understand (vv. 23-25).

This third section has various speakers, as did the first, while the second had only one—the people, just as the central section in the first foe cycle had only one speaker—Yahweh.

f. The Relation of the Supplementary Foe Cycle to the First Foe Cycle

I have already touched on many details that concern the relation of this supplementary foe cycle to the first foe cycle: (1) the reversal of the pattern of single-imperative and multiple-imperative sections (see 6, a); (2) the symmetry of single-speaker and multiple-speaker sections (see 6, e); (3) the "inside-out" structure of the interlude in comparison to that of the prelude and postlude of the first foe cycle (see 6, c); and (4) the general sense one has that the situation has grown more desperate (see 6, a). But there are some further observations now that need to be made.

The close of the first foe cycle (*i.e.*, the postlude there, 8:4ff) held echoes of the first half of the harlotry cycle in Jer. 2. The parallel echo in the supplementary foe cycle, we found, was in the interlude. Since that link has already been achieved, the end of the supplementary foe cycle simply echoes the *prelude* to the first foe cycle. In this way a kind of rough symmetry or parity is maintained. If we assign arbitrary letters to the landmarks along the way, the scheme might look something like this:

the call (chap. 1)	—A
seed oracle, and harlotry cycle, first half (chap. 2)	—A′B
prelude to first foe cycle (4:1-4)	—C
first foe cycle proper (4:5ff)	—D
postlude to first foe cycle (8:4ff)	—B′C′
suppl. foe cycle (8:14ff)	—D′
interlude	—B″
coda to suppl. foe cycle (10:23-25)	—A″C″

The supplementary foe cycle is then just that—a supplement. The first foe cycle has, in its conclusion, integrated itself well into the totality of the harlotry and foe cycles; the supplementary foe cycle manages to do the same, and still to give the impression moving forward to fresh ground.

It is striking that the first foe cycle has seven sections and the supplementary foe cycle has three sections, for a total of ten. These numbers—seven, three, and ten—are numbers that figure often in biblical tradition: one thinks of the seven sons and three daughters of Job (Job 1:2, 42:13),[21] Job's seven thousand sheep and three thousand camels (Job 1:3; in 42:12 these totals are doubled!), and Solomon's seven hundred wives and three hundred concubines (1 Kings 11:3). Beyond the Old Testament literature proper, one finds in the (Ethiopian) book of Enoch, chapter 93, seven "weeks" of past history, and in 91:12-17, three "weeks" of future history, before the new heaven and new earth come. It is altogether attractive, therefore, to see this pattern here.[22]

g. A Note on Secondary Insertions (9:11-15; 9:22-25; 10:1-16)

Little need be said about this material, which is universally taken as secondary. The material in 9:11-15 is plainly midrashic, explaining in catechetical fashion how it is that one can speak in the terms of 9:9.

Verses 22-23 are a wisdom unit. I suggest they are placed here because the key word is the verb *ḥpṣ*, "delight," v. 23. The only previous occurrence of this verb is in 6:10,[23] where it is followed (in 6:11) by the phrase *'ōlāl* plus preposition plus *ḥûṣ* ("children in the street"), in parallel with *baḥûrîm* ("young men"). This phraseological parallelism appears here in 9:20;[24] therefore a passage with *ḥpṣ* is inserted here.

Similarly, vv. 24-25 are here because of the key words *'ărēlîm/'arlē/'orlâ*, since 6:10 (see the previous paragraph) has *ʿărēlâ* ("their ear is uncircumcised").[25] This is to say that we have the following scheme:

6:10 — "uncircumcised"
— "pleasure"
6:11 — "children in the street, young men. . . ."

Therefore two orphan passages, one with "pleasure" and one with "uncircumcised," are inserted (in chiastic order!) after 9:21, the end of a unit containing "children in the street, young men. . . ." These are examples of what I shall call "adjunction by preexisting association"; we have seen a similar instance already,[26] and we shall see more.

The poem against idolatry (10:1-16), whether or not genuine to Jeremiah,[27] is obviously intrusive here. I would suggest that it is inserted here because of the verb "learn" in v. 2 (*lmd* qal), after "teach" (*lmd* piel) in 9:19 (and 9:4).[28]

7

The Material in Chapters 11-20

a. The Problem of Analysis, and the Search for Method

As we may readily see, the material in chapters 11-20 is far more varied than that of chapters 2-10. This section of the book gives every evidence of having been compiled at several stages, the compilers feeling quite free to insert new material as seemed best at the time. These insertions were made on the basis of catchword links and of other associative devices that seemed appropriate, but the problem for the analyst is that while one can often see the catchword or thought-links, it is not so easy to decide whether a link identifies a literary unit as belonging to a first stage, second stage, or subsequent stage in the growing corpus. It is a matter of some delicacy, therefore, to develop for the growth of the corpus a model that gives some conviction of being the correct one.

The issue is exemplified by what may be called the "cursed be the man" question, already discussed in the introduction (b). The data of the occurrence of this phrase—three times, twice with *'îš* (11:3, 20:15), once with *geber* (17:5)—are plain; and the suspicion of the rhetorical significance of the phrase (justified, as I shall suggest) is insistent. But how to develop a model of the growth of chapters 11-20 from such data? Many such problems will emerge, and we shall simply have to work out the most satisfactory model, but often with a greater tentativeness than was felt necessary in dealing with chapters 1-10.

There is a problem also of the fashion by which the model is here presented: if one works through the material of chapters 11-20 chapter by chapter, then the analysis would become inefficient and confusing, but if one presents the model before any chapter-by-chapter analysis, then it would appear that the solution is offered *a priori.* I shall steer a middle course, suggesting the solution with some confirming evidence, and then plunging into the material more or less chapter by chapter to strengthen the argumentation.

b. The Hypothesis: The Initial Stratum of Chapters 11-20—Confessional and Quasi-Confessional Material; The Two Integrating Passages (16:1-9 and 20:14-18)

Once one gets past the initial impression of *variety* in the material of chapters 11-20, he notes the presence of two new genres—the so-called confessions, which seem to begin with 11:18 and end with 20:18, and symbolic actions—the waistcloth in 13:1-11, the encounter with the potter in 18:1-11, the pottery flask in 19:1-15, and the perhaps related incident of the change of Pashhur's name in 20:1-6.

It may be helpful to describe at this point a *false* hypothesis with which I began some time ago, namely, that the organization of this section of material might be based upon an *alternation* of these confessional and symbolic-action passages; I assumed at that point that the call to celibacy (16:1-9) was in the category of symbolic actions. I mention this false lead because I think it important that the analyst not assume *a priori* that the initial stratum of material must contain poetry exclusively, rather than narrative, or rather than some kind of intermixture of genres. The question, as always, must be: what makes the most plausible model of the rhetorical data before us?

(Here let me define the term *initial stratum* just used. By *initial stratum* I mean, quite simply, the earliest material in a given section of the book of Jeremiah, material that was then incorporated into the growing collection of Jeremianic material. The term does *not* imply a *single* stage in the collection process; *i.e.,* the initial stratum of chapters 11-16 probably took shape [and indeed was probably incorporated into the material of chapters 1-10] before the initial stratum of chapters 17-20 took shape.)

It seems, then, after all, that it is the confessional poetry that forms the initial stratum of this section of the book of Jeremiah. And this is a reasonable assumption; if a Jeremianic corpus began with the call in chapter 1, and if Jeremiah's own relation to Yahweh was an issue for him at some point, then it is plausible that a collection of the material setting forth his intercourse with Yahweh could balance (in an inclusio) the call-narrative in chapter 1, bracketing the oracles of judgment in the harlotry and foe cycles.

But we must not assume too quickly that the initial stratum consists of what the commentators have traditionally reckoned to be the "confessions"; we shall continue to search for rhetorical clues.

Is there any rhetorical hint at the beginning of the confessional material as to the contents of the initial stratum of material (in the way that the seed oracle, 2:2-3, anticipated the contents of chapters 2-6)? There is not. Indeed, the first confession (11:18ff) begins without warning or introduction—might seem, in fact, to have close links with the end of chapter 10 ("know" twice in 11:18, linked with occurrences in 10:23 and 25), so that, as we have seen, Hyatt took 10:23-24 to be confessional.[1] There is symmetry within the material in 11:18-12:6, as we shall see, but beyond that passage the first link that strikes fire with us is that between "your [=Jeremiah's] father" in 12:6 and "my [=Jeremiah's] mother" in 15:10, at the beginning of what seems to be (and is, as I shall shortly demonstrate) the next passage of confessional material. This link is not fortuitous, but a major key to the unlocking of the structure of this section of the book of Jeremiah. I shall call 11:18-12:6 the "father" complex, and 15:10-21 the "mother" complex, postponing the question as to whether each of these sequences is a unit or multiple. (More accurately, these complexes are made up respectively of 11:18-12:3, 5-6—since v. 4 is secondary, though added early[2]—and 15:10-12, 15-21, since vv. 13-14 are secondary.) The basic point to be made at this time, however, is that there is nothing at the beginning of the "father" complex and the "mother" complex to correspond in function with the seed oracle in 2:2-3.

The surprise, in fact, is that we have the opposite—that is, oracles that *round off* the material, summarizing, or, as I shall term it, "integrating" it, at the end of a given sequence of material rather than at the beginning. There are two of these integrating passages—two passages that use "father" and "mother" in ways that imply a rhetorical function: 16:1-9 and 20:14-18. Let us take 20:14-18 first. Here we find reference again to Jeremiah's father and mother—indeed, 12:6, 15:10, and 20:14-18 are the *only* passages containing direct poetic references to Jeremiah's father and/or mother in the whole book.[3] Indeed, the verb forms associated with "mother" in 15:10 and 20:14 are closely linked as well —*yᵉlidtînî* in 15:10, and *yᵉlādatnî* in 20:14, corresponding to the needs of second-person vocative and third-person reference respectively.

But the earlier passage referred to, 16:1-9, also uses "father" and "mother" in a way that implies a rhetorical function for the passage. Here the references are not to the prophet's own father and mother, but the occurrences are symmetrical: "the mothers who bore (*hayyōlᵉdôt*) them and the fathers who begot (*hammôlîdîm*) them," 16:3; and "his father and his mother," 16:7, with reversal of order. I have argued elsewhere[4] for the poetic structure of this passage; now I contend that this passage itself functions rhetorically to integrate the confessional material that has just preceded it—the father complex and the mother complex.

If we lay these two "integrating" passages side by side, we note that besides references to father and mother, they share two more roots—*qbr* and *śmḥ: yiqqābᵉrû,* 16:4, 6, and *qibrî*, 20:17; *śammēaḥ śimmᵒḥāhû*, 20:15. (I would even suggest that the *cross-patterning of verbs and nouns* here is part of the symmetry.) Now, if both these passages do indeed have an integrating function, then we would expect both these roots to occur in previous material. For *śmh* the occurrence is obvious: *śimḥâ*, the same word as in 16:9, appears in the "mother" complex, 15:16 (*ûlᵉśimḥat*). By symmetry, then, we would expect the root *qbr* to appear somewhere in the father complex.

It does not, but a search reveals *qārôb,* "near," in 12:2.

Is it possible that the occurrences of *qbr* in 16:4, 6, and 20:17 echo *qārôb* by permutation of the consonants? Evidently so, because the companion of *qārôb,* namely, *rāḥôq,* "far," is echoed by one of the companions of *yiqqāberû* in 16:6, namely, *yiqqārēaḥ*, "be shaved bald," again by permutation of consonants. That is to say, two adjectives in semantic balance in 12:2 are matched by two verbs in semantic balance in 16:6 by permutation of their respective consonants! This stunning parallelism can scarcely be coincidental.

Let us now complete the analysis of the links between the father complex, the mother complex, and the integrating passage, 16:1-9. We notice that the links between the father complex and 16:1-9 are found in the "funeral" section (*i.e.*, the *qbr-qrḥ* parallel in 16:6), while the link already noticed between the mother complex and 16:1-9 is found in the "wedding" section (*i.e.,* *śāśôn,* 15:16 and 16:9, and two first-person verbs, *wā'ōkelēm*, and I ate them, 15:16, and *yāšabtî,* I sat, twice, 15:17, on the one hand, and their infinitives, *lāšebet* and *le'ekōl*, in 16:8 (in reverse order!).

To summarize: there are links between the father complex and the funeral section of 16:1-9, and there are links between the mother complex and the wedding section of 16:1-9. There are no links of which I am aware between 16:1-9 and any previous material between 11:18 and the end of chapter 15 except for the two complexes discussed; in particular, there is no evidence of any echoes to the drought complex, 14:1ff. It would seem a reasonable hypothesis, then, that 16:1-9 rounded off 11:18-12:6 and 15:10-21.

Now let us return to 20:14-18 for closer examination. The first verse, v. 14, contains the two passive participles *'ārûr* and *bārûk*; these evidently echo 17:5 and 7 respectively.[5] But the word to which the participles are linked, *hayyôm,* does not appear in 17:5ff; instead, we find *bišnat* in 17:8. When one looks through the material in 17:14-20:13, one finds three occurrences of *yôm,* 17:16-18, then an occurrence of *beʿēt* in 18:23, and then two occurrences of *hayyôm* in 20:7-8, which seem to correspond to *hayyôm, beʿēt, yāmay* respectively in 20:14, 16, 18.[6] But there is more: if we look back into the initial stratum of chapters 11-15 (*i.e.,* the father complex and the mother complex) to locate words for time, we find *šenat* in 11:23, *leyôm* in 12:3, and *beʿēt* twice in 15:11. If we line these up now side by side, we find some very striking parallels:

11:23 *šenat peqquddātām*	17:8 *ûbišnat baṣṣōret*	
12:3 *leyôm haregâ*	17:16 *weyôm ʾānûš* 17:17 *beyôm rāʿâ* 17:18 *yôm rāʿâ*	20:14 *ʾārûr hayyôm*
15:11 *beʿēt rāʿâ* *ûbeʿēt ṣārâ*	18:23 *beʿēt ʾappekā*	20:16 *beʿēt ṣohorāyim*
	20:7 *kol-hayyôm* 20:8 *kol-hayyôm*	20:18 *yāmay*

If one assigns "A" to *šānâ,* "B" to *yôm,* "C" to *ʿēt,* and "D" to *yôm* again, then one finds the sequence A-B-C, A-B-C-D, B-C-D in the occurrence of these words, and one is struck by the assonantal association of *ṣārâ*, "distress," 15:11, *baṣṣōret*, "drought," 17:8, and *ṣohorāyim*, "noon," 20:16. (Question: are these words further reflections of the *mibṣār/bōṣēr/māṣôr* assonance in the two foe cycles?) We may note in passing that the sequence in the first column, together with other symmetries elucidated in 7d, make unlikely any rearrangement of the verses of 11:18-12:6 as many commentators suggest.[7]

In any event, the sequence of *yôm* and *'ēt* in the "confessional" material of chapters 17-20 is paralleled by the sequence in 20:14-18, so that I shall call these confessional passages—17:14-18, 18:18-23, 20:7-13—the day complex.

Likewise, as we have seen, the phrase *'ārûr hā'îš 'ᵃšer* in 20:15, with *bārûk* in 20:14, reflects *'ārûr haggeber 'ᵃšer* in 17:5 and *bārûk haggeber 'ᵃšer* in 17:7. We note further that 20:15 continues with the verb *biśśar,* "brought (good) news to," which is evidently an echo of *bāśar,* "[makes] flesh [his arm]" in 17:5. These ties press us to see 17:5ff as a part of the initial stratum that is rounded off by 20:14-18; we shall see later that the passage evidently ends with 17:10. The inclusion of 17:5ff among the so-called confessions is a surprise;[8] later I shall justify its inclusion in this category on the basis of both content and structure, but for the moment we should note that the passage shares much with 11:18-12:6—both 17:5-8 and 12:2 are modeled in different ways on Psalm 1, and thus both passages share the vocabulary of trees (*'ēṣ, nṭ',* "root," "fruit"). I shall call 17:5-10 the man complex (though admitted it is not very complex!) in order to set it into parallel with the day complex and the earlier ones.

We can now see that there is a precise symmetry in the *arrangement* of the indicators in 20:14-15 with respect to the arrangement of the complexes in chapters 11-20, which I have hypothesized: the pairs are dovetailed and the order of each member reversed:

We recall the two roots that 16:1-9 and 20:14-18 manifested in common beyond "father" and "mother," namely, *qbr* and *śmḥ,* and we recall the symmetry by which *qbr* in the funeral section of 16:1-9 echoes a word in the father complex and *śmh* in the wedding section of

11:18-12:6	—"father" (12:6)
15:10-21	— "mother" (15:10)
17:5-10	— "cursed be the man . . . .flesh (*bāśār*)" (17:5)
17:14-18	— "day" (17:17, 18)
18:18-23	— "time" (18:23)
20:7-13	— "day" (20:7, 8)

20:14	— "day" (+ "time," v. 16, "days" v. 18)
	— "mother"
20:15	— "cursed be the man who brought good news *(biśśar)*"
	— "father"

16:1-9 echoed a word in the mother complex. Now, in 20:14-18 we see the associations with "father" and "mother" reversed: it is the father in 20:15 who is made very glad by the news of Jeremiah's birth, and it is the mother in 20:17 who would have been Jeremiah's grave.

The passage 20:14-18 is essentially chiastic in arrangement:

v. 14:	"day"			
	"day"			
		"mother"		
v. 15:			"man"	
v. 16:				"cities"
			3rd-pers. ref. = "man"	
v. 17:		"mother"		
v. 18:	"days."			

This being the case, its positional mapping, as we might term it, of the previous complexes, is all the more remarkable.

There are several other word- or sound-echoes to these complexes, or to earlier material in chapters 1-10, that I might mention: *babbōqer* in 20:16 is another variation on the *qbr* combination; *raḥmāh,* the companion of *qibrî* in v. 17 (and indeed the other two occurrences of *reḥem* in vv. 17-18 as well), might be a partial echo of the *qrḥ* combination in 12:2 and 16:6, with two consonants in common if not three. And *bᵉbōšet* in v. 18 (pronounced *bᵉbošt*) is perhaps an echo of *lāšebet* (pronounced *lāšibt*) in 16:8; we recall the *bwš-šwb-bwš* sequence in Jer. 2-3.

But there are three or four more echoes of earlier material in 20:14-18, all of them in 20:16—and these all point to 15:5-8:

nḥm – *nḥm* (15:6)
za'ᵃqâ — *za'ᵃqâ* (15:5)
'ārîm — *îr* II, "agitation" (15:8)?
ṣohᵒrayim — *ṣohᵒrayim* (15:8).

A check with a concordance will indicate that these words do not turn up elsewhere in 11:18-20:13.[9] We shall have to wait until I analyze the drought complex (7,e) to see the significance of these echoes, for I shall have first to demonstrate that 15:5-9 was part of the drought complex. But we shall see later (7, d, 7, e) that 12:4 was evidently not originally a part of 12:1-6, but added at the time the drought complex was integrated into the growing corpus. Since the echoes in 12:4 are to the *beginning* of the drought complex (*i.e.*, 14:1-6) and the echoes here in 20:16 are to material at the *end* (or after the end, depending upon how we define its extent), there is good reason to believe that at the time the man complex, the day complex, and the closing integrating passage (20:14-18) were added to the growing corpus, the drought complex had been inserted between the father complex and the mother complex, and 12:4 had been inserted in its place.

Though we shall be looking at confirmatory evidence, passage by passage, in chapters 11-20, I may perhaps allow myself a few reactions and provisional conclusions to this model, if it seems a valid one.

First, it comes as a great surprise to us that 20:14-18, the most agonized of Jeremiah's outbursts, turns out also to have this curious "mapping" function, indicating what has come before in this particular collection. Of course a fugue of Bach's, or a sonnet of Shakespeare's, can bring high emotion into strict structure; nevertheless, if the chiasmus does not surprise us, the "integrating" function does.

Second, we are startled by the echoes and wordplay across a distance of several chapters, such as both 16:1-9 and 20:14-18 offer us, just as we were startled by similar echoes across a distance of several chapters in the material of chapters 1-10.

Third, I have already expressed surprise at the inclusion of 17:5ff (as we shall see, the passage is 17:5-10) with the initial stratum (the "confessions") of chapters 17-20; and the function of 16:1-9 as a "map" of the initial stratum of chapters 11-15 is just as surprising. Neither 16:1-9 nor 17:5-8 has been reckoned among the "confessions"; indeed, many commentators have doubted the authenticity of some of 16:1-9, and all of 17:5-10.[10] But if the guidance of the rhetorical links between the "confessions proper" on the one hand, and 16:1-9 and 20:14-18 on the other, is to be trusted, then it looks as if the material is incorporated in the early stages of the growing corpus. I shall later suggest in an exegesis of 17:5-8 (7, i) that this passage is a true "confession"; and after all, both 16:1-9 and 17:9-10 come under the rubric of "Jeremiah's intercourse with Yahweh," in which his fellow-citizens appear, when they appear at all, simply as enemies of Yahweh and are not addressed, appealed to, or reckoned with in the context of historical events. There is, then, a general unity of content to the material that I have been discussing.

Fourth, we note (as I pointed out in the Introduction, b) that 16:1-9 and 20:14-18 are not form-critically parallel at all: 16:1-9 is a narrative of Yahweh's call to Jeremiah, quite analogous to that of chapter 1, while 20:14-18, a confessional utterance, is Jeremiah's lament to Yahweh. Nevertheless, both passages have a parallel *rhetorical* function.

Fifth, 15:15-21, 16:1-9, and 20:14-18 all offer echoes of the structure of chapters 1-10. (a) As we shall see when we take a closer look at 15:15-21, 15:19 contains a symmetrical quadruple *šwb* in a way that implies an echo of both the double *šwb* of the prelude and the double *šwb* of the postlude of the first foe cycle (see 7,d). (b) The last word in 16:9 is *kallâ,* "bride," suggesting a kind of recapitulation that goes back to chapter 2. (c) Most substantially, both integrating passages, each in its own way, offer an inclusio to the call-narrative of chapter 1—this has been implied in much of what I have said, but we should now take a closer look at the situation. As for 20:14-18, the whole passage implies a rejection of the call, and the phrases in the passage of course echo 1:5 (as we noted in the use of *reḥem*). This suggests an inclusio for the whole of the material in chapters 1-20 at the stage when 20:14-18 would complete it.[11] But 16:1-9, like 20:14-18, echoes in its own way the call-narrative of chapter 1: the introductory words in 1:4 and 16:1 are identical, but more substantially, the passage is a kind of second call. Some have argued that *na'ar* in chapter 1 means "bachelor."[12] If there is merit in this suggestion, then 16:1-9 confirms Jeremiah's bachelor status and makes the objection of 1:6 ("I am only a youth") into a permanent sign. In any event, if 16:1-9 has the rhetorical function here of integrating, as I suggest, then it would explain the otherwise rather puzzling position of this passage deep within the book of Jeremiah, for it *is* a puzzle why we should have to wait until chapter 16 to learn that Jeremiah should never marry.

Now that this model has been set forth, however, we must go back and establish both the existence and the extent of the complexes suggested by the patterning of the proposed "integrating passage," by a detailed examination of chapters 11-20.

c. A Preliminary Survey of the Material in Chapters 11-16

Let us begin by a preliminary survey of the material from chapters 11 through 16, since 16:1-9 seems to round off the initial stratum of chapters 11-15. The prose passage 11:1-17 seems, on superficial examination, to be of the same type as the prose passage in 7:1-8:3: many of the same stereotyped Deuteronomistic phrases appear. But whereas at least a portion of the 7:1-8:3 turned out to offer variations on themes of 6:16-21, the material in 11:1-7 has no apparent connection with anything that precedes it; instead, as seems to be indicated by the parallelism between 11:3 and 20:15, the passage serves as a kind of introduction to the new section of the book. And because it is basically prose material, and because it points so far toward the end of the section, in chapter 20, we suspect that it is a latecomer on the scene and that it gives no help in discerning the pattern of the earlier stages of chapters 11-20. I will discuss it in 7, k.

There follows, as is well known, the first "confession" (11:18ff). Confessional material continues through 12:6, to be followed by a poem (12:7-13) that is evidently a lament of Yahweh over Judah (this is a new genre!), followed by secondary material (12:14-17). Then comes another new type—a symbolic action, the incident of the waistcloth (13:1-11). A great variety of material follows, including the complex about a drought and related material (14:1ff). Confessional material seems to begin again in 15:10, and continues through 15:21.

I have already taken note of the possibility that 15:19 echoes the prelude and postlude of the first foe cycle, and we shall see more reminiscences in 15:15-21 of material in the early part of the book; we have already examined in detail the integrating function of 16:1-9.

The remainder of chapter 16 contains demonstrably secondary material: even 16:16-18 and 16:19-20 were inserted at a later stage, as we shall see.

d. The Father and Mother Complexes (11:18-12:3, 5-6; 15:10-12, 15-21), Closed by the Integrating Call to Celibacy (16:1-9)

When we reach 11:18 we are dealing with material that appears to form a natural succession to 10:23-25, as noted above (7, b): 10:23 begins with *yāda'tî*, and 11:18 with *hôdî'anî wā'ēda'â*, continuing in v. 19 with *yāda'tî*. Since, however, 1:5 has *yᵉda'tîka*, one senses that 11:18 is not only linked with 10:23-25, but marks the beginning of a new collection that will be in parallel (indeed is in inclusio) with the call in chapter 1.

In this first "confession," 11:18-20 obviously presents Jeremiah's words to Yahweh, and vv. 21-23 Yahweh's answer. I suggest that vv. 22-23 embody poetry:

v. 22:	*hin^{e}nî pōqēd ʿ^{a}lêhem*	behold I am visiting upon them
	habbaḥûrîm yāmūtû baḥereb	their chosen shall die by sword
	b^{e}nêhem [ûb^{e}nôtêhem] yāmūtû bārāʿāb	their sons [and their daughters] shall die by famine
v.23:	*ûš^{e}'ērit lō' tihyeh lāhem*	and a remnant shall not be to them
	kî-'ābî' rāʿâ	for I shall bring disaster
	'el-'anšê ʿ^{a}nātôt	to the men of Anathoth
	š^{e}nat p^{e}quddātām	(in) the year of their visitation.

We note the inclusio of *pqd,* the assonance of *baḥûrîm* and *baḥereb,* the repetition of *yāmūtû,* the assonance of ʿ^{a}*lêhem* and *lāhem*, of *rāʿāb* and *rāʿâ*, and the reversal of consonants in *'anšê* and *š^{e}nat*. Question: the word *ûb^{e}nôtêhem* seems extra here: was it an *addition* when 16:1-9 became part of the corpus?—16:2, 3 offer "sons and daughters" as a parallel to "mothers and fathers," and to "bridegroom and bride" in 16:9.

The next poem, 12:1-3, offers a second "confession" of Jeremiah's; vv. 5-6 bring the second answer from God. For a discussion of v. 4, see 7,e.

I have already presented data suggesting that "your father" in 12:6 was followed, in the earliest stage of the tradition, by "my mother" in 15:10; the parallel mention of Jeremiah's father and mother in 20:14-15, and the symmetry of references to "father" and "mother" in 16:3 and 7; and the possibility that *ûb^{e}nôtêhem* in 11:22 was added as the "female" material 15:10-16:9 was added to the corpus, all point in this direction.

One other thought: let us recall the possibility that *'ābî* in 3:4 implies "my husband," and served as a balance to *k^{e}lûlôtayik* in 2:2, "your bridehood."[13] Do we have here a partial parallel: "your father" in 12:6 and "my mother" in 15:10? In 2:2 Yahweh addresses Israel, and in 3:4 the vocative is conceived of as the address of Israel to

Yahweh. In 12:6 the reference is to Jeremiah's father, while in 15:10 Jeremiah offers an apostrophe to his mother. The parallel is of course not exact: Jeremiah's parents do not address each other here as Yahweh and Israel address each other in chapters 2 and 3; but there is sexual complementarity, and symmetry of possessive suffixes, in both pairs, leading us to wonder whether the material in the initial stratum of chapters 11-15 took shape in part as a parallel to chapters 2-3.

Evidence will be given below that the assignments of speaker in 15:10-21 are divided between Jeremiah (v. 10), Yahweh (vv. 11-12), Jeremiah (vv. 15-18), and Yahweh (vv. 19-21) in a plan wholly parallel to that of 11:18-12:6. The two halves of 11:18-12:6 and the two halves of 15:10-21 are arranged chiastically in their key words:

11:18-23: *hôdî'anî wā'ēdā'â* (11:18),
yāda'tî (11:19)

nqm (11:20)

12:1-3,
5-6: "your father" (12:6)

15:10-12: "my mother" (15:10)

15:15-21: *yāda'tā* (15:15)
nqm (15:15).

Such symmetry is certainly reassuring.

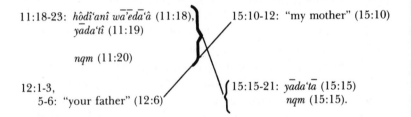

I have already spoken several times of the link *(yd')* between 10:23-25 and 11:18-19. There are a few other links between the material in these first two complexes and material in the last subdivision of the supplementary foe cycle (10:17-25): one notes *'ôy lî* in 10:19 and 15:10[14] and *makkātî* in 10:19 and 15:18.[15] Further, the very pattern of dialogue between Yahweh and the people in 10:19ff, involving as it does a lament on the part of the people (not to mention the dialogical quality of all the material in the foe cycles), helps to make plausible the confessional material in 11:18ff.

I have also already spoken of the link provided by *yd'* between 11:18-19 and 1:5, in the call, and suggested that the confessional material (in dealing with the relationship between Jeremiah and Yahweh) is a suitable body of material to make up an inclusio with the call. But there are more specific links of this sort: *l*e*haṣṣîlekā* in 1:8 and 15:20, and "I ate [thy words]" 15:16 and "my mouth" 15:19 reflecting "I have put my words in your mouth," 1:9. There are links with the seed oracle, 2:2-3: the verb *zkr* in 15:15 ("remember me") recalls 2:2 ("I remember the devotion of your youth")[16] and *'ābî' rā'â 'al* recalls 2:3 and its parallels in the foe cycle.[17]

But the most striking of such reminiscences is the quadruple *šwb* in 15:19, part of Yahweh's answer to Jeremiah: *'im-tāšûb wa'ašîbekā. . .yāšûbû hēmmâ 'ēlêkā w*e*'attâ lō'-tāšûb 'alêhem*, which (mathematically!) balances the double use of *šwb* in both the prelude and postlude of the first foe cycle, combining the phraseology (*'im-, tāšûb, 'el-, yāšûb-, w*e*lō'*) of both passages (4:1: *'im-tāšûb. . .'ēlay tāšûb*; 8:4 *'im-yāšûb w*e*lō' yāšûb*), and so recalls for us not only the first foe cycle but the linkage (by *šwb*) to chapter 3 as well.

Let us now return to the individual complexes and pick up some details. The two laments of Jeremiah in the "father" complex are chiastically arranged with respect to each other:[18]

11:18: *yhwh, hôdî'anî, hir'îtanî*[19]
11:19: "lamb" (*'allûp*), *litbôaḥ*
"tree" (*'ēṣ*)
11:20: yhwh, *šōpēt ṣedeq*
rîb

12:1 *ṣaddîq, yhwh*
'arîb, mišpat
12:2: "plant" *(nṭ')*
12:3: *yhwh, y^eda'tanî, tir'enî*
"sheep" *(ṣo'n)*, *l^etibḥâ.*

We are justified, then, on structural grounds as well as on the ground of contents, in excising v. 4 as secondary (with most commentators); when I discuss the drought complex (7, e), I shall make a suggestion as to the way by which 12:4 became part of the poem.

Verses 1-2 are Jeremiah's personal variation on Psalm 1; this fact will become important as we come to consider 17:5-8 (7, i).

The second answer from Yahweh (12:5-6) is linked with the first (11:21-23) by the phrases "their sons" (11:22) and "men of Anathoth" (11:23) on the one hand, and "your brothers and the house of your father" (12:6) on the other, and the second answer is linked with the second lament by the words *bgd* and *dbr* piel (12:1 and 6).[20]

Now 15:10ff. Verses 11-12 have caused much difficulty to commentators and translators. I would suggest that the MT can be made to yield good sense, but I must offer an exegesis of the passage in order to justify the structural assumptions that I have already made.

On the surface, v. 10 is an address not to Yahweh but to the prophet's mother; but a complaint to Yahweh is plainly implied: Jeremiah's birth is associated with his call (1:5), and, as I hope to show, it is Yahweh who answers in vv. 11-12. We note that the noun *rîb* (v. 10) echoes the same noun in the first "confession" (11:20) (and the corresponding verb in 12:1).[21]

As for verse 11, most commentators and translators

follow the LXX ("Amen, O Lord. . ."), making v. 11 a continuation of Jeremiah's address,[22] and most vocalize *šrwtk* as *šēratfīkā* (*srt* piel, "serve").[23]

On the contrary, I would follow the MT. Jeremiah has been talking (at least figuratively) to his mother; but Yahweh answers. Now, the best parallel to the phrase *hipga'tî b^eka 'et-* is found in Isa. 53:6: "And Yahweh laid on him (*hipgî^a' bô 'et-*) the iniquity of us all." Isa. 53 here imitates Jeremiah's confessions; note that 53:7 is parallel to Jer. 11:18. So the phrase in Jeremiah means: "I have laid on you—the foe." Then, by parallelism, *šrwtk* must have something to do with being an enemy. The obvious solution is the word *šōrer,* "enemy," in the Psalms (five times: 5:9, 27:11, 54:7, 56:3, 59:11), always in the form *sōr^eray/-ay*, "my enemies". Jeremiah would take this word in the Psalms as the participle of a verb *šrr:* either he made up an *ad hoc* verb, or else he has given us another cited form of the verb than the participle, and the verb would then be *šārōfīkā,* exactly what the consonantal text demands. So this means "I have 'enemied' you for the best, I have laid upon you, in a time of disaster and in a time of distress, the foe!" Essentially, then, this answer from God is analogous to that of 12:5-6: "Jeremiah, I know exactly what I am doing."

I even suggest that v. 12 can be understood. Let us go back to 12:5: "If you have run with men on foot and then have wearied you, how will you compete with horses?" I would suggest that there is a very specific reference in this verse. Who "runs," considering Jeremiah's vocabulary? The qal of *rwṣ* appears three times in the book of Jeremiah: here, in 23:21, and in 51:31. In the last passage the reference is to official "runners." In 23:21 the reference, surprisingly enough, is to the (false) prophets: "I did not send the prophets, yet they ran; I did not speak to them, yet they prophesied."[24] Is the reference in 12:5 to Jeremiah's competition with the false prophets?[25] "Horses" of course suggests the military might of the foe from the north. Does 12:5 suggest that Jeremiah's main difficulty will come from the foreign invasion, not from domestic rivals in the prophetic office?

If so, I suggest that 15:12 has the same implication. The text may stand as it is: Jeremiah elsewhere offers cola in which the second and third words are identical.[26] The phrase *barzel miṣṣāpôn,* like "horses" in 12:5, is an expression for the military prowess of the enemy. The remaining phrase, *barzel. . .ûnᵉḥōšet,* represents the old poetic pattern of the "break-up of stereotyped phrases," so many examples of which Mitchell Dahood was found in the Psalms.[27] At the end of the first foe cycle the people are called "bronze and iron" (6:28), so again, as in 12:5, the contrast seems to be between the people who rebel against Yahweh at home, and the enemy from abroad. Then 15:12, with its ambiguity of subject and object, would seem to mean: "Who will break whom?—iron from the north [the foreign foe] or iron and bronze [the rebellious people]?" Yahweh is suggesting that Jeremiah turn his attention away from domestic enemies to the foreign threat.

Verses 13-14 do not belong here; they are secondarily inserted from 17:3b-4,[28] on the association of "iron and bronze" (15:12) and "iron and *šāmîr*" (17:1), in much the same way as that by which 8:10b-12 was inserted (see 4, o).

Now, we have already seen that 11:18-23 and 12:1-6 are related to each other chiastically; I may remark here that there is a link between the two halves of the mother complex—"bronze" (15:12, 20).

Nothing more need be said about 15:15-21; we have seen how this material fits into place in the structure of the two confessional complexes here proposed.

Nor need much more be said about the call to celibacy (16:1-9), since I have elsewhere discussed its poetic structure[29] and have already analyzed its integrating function with respect to the two confessional complexes that precede it.

e. The Drought Complex (14:1-15:9)

We now turn to an extended complex that has long been recognized to be a literary unit: the material on the drought.[30] There is a difference of opinion as to whether the complex ends with 15:4 (so most commentators) or with 15:9 (so Cornill, Reventlow).[31] The material divides into a description of a drought (14:2-6), a communal lament (14:7-9), followed by Yahweh's response (14:10); conversation then ensues between Yahweh and Jeremiah over the situation (14:11-18, according to the usual reckoning);[32] then a second communal lament (14:19-22) followed by Yahweh's response (15:1-4). And if we reckon 15:5-9 with the complex, 15:5 is a lament by the prophet, followed by Yahweh's response (15:6-9). (I shall give evidence below, from analysis by rhetorical criticism, that 15:5-9 does indeed belong with the complex.) Whatever may have been the process by which this complex took shape (and here form-criticism can come to our aid), rhetorically we are justified in dealing with the material as a totality, as we shall see.

The description of the drought (14:2-6) looks like a self-standing poem. When we move to examine the first communal lament, we suspect a double meaning in *miqweh* (14:8)—normally translated "hope," but perhaps meaning "pool" as well.[33] There follows Yahweh's reply, hinting that it is the people who are the wanderers rather than he (v. 10).

The unit vv. 11-12 (whether it might be trimmed to poetic form or not) is here, at least in part, because of the link "I will not accept them" (*'ênennî roṣam,* v. 12) with "does not accept them" (*lō' raṣam,* v. 10).[34] The unit vv. 13-16 is of course here because of "sword and famine"; vv. 17-18 are also present because of "sword" and "famine"—and "prophet" as well (cf. vv. 13-15). (The likeness in phraseology between 14:17 and 13:17 is evidently not germane to the question of the position of this unit.)

Verses 19-22 bring a second lament, and there are several word-linkages with vv. 7-9: *'āwôn* (vv. 7, 20); *lᵉkā ḥāṭā'nû* (v. 7), *ḥāṭā'nû lāk* (v. 20); *šimkā* (vv. 9, 21); *miqweh* (v. 8), *nᵉqawweh-llāk* (v. 22); and indeed an echo of vv. 2-6: *magšimîm,* "bringing rain" (v. 22), *gešem* (v. 4).

The response of Yahweh in 15:1-4 is in content more like 14:11-12 than like 14:10, but in any case it is a response to 14:19-22 (*napšî* in 15:1 echoes *napšekā* in 14:19).

There are several instances of inclusio between 15:5-9 and 14:2-6: forms of *šaʿᵃrîm*, "gates," 14:2 and 15:7, with no intervening occurrences;[35] the verb *bwš*, 14:4 (and 3?) and 15:9, with no intervening occurrences; *yālᵉdâ*, 14:5, and *yōledet*, 15:9, with no intervening occurrences; and, most strikingly, *'umlᵉlû*, "languish," 14:2, and *'umlᵉlâ*, 15:9, the only two occurrences of this verb in Jeremiah.

But if 15:5-9 seems to close off the drought complex, it would also seem to offer catchwords by which the material is linked to 15:10ff: "mother of a young man," 15:8, and "my mother," 15:10; the verb *yld,* vv. 9, 10.[36]

But if 15:5-9 is integrated by theme and catchwords to the mother complex that follows, is there a way by which the beginning of the drought complex is linked to the father complex that precedes? There is; the link is supplied by 12:4, the verse that did not "belong" in the passage at the earliest stage because it broke the chiastic pattern of 11:18-20 and 12:1-3 (see above, 7,d): we find *'ēśeb* 12:4 and 14:6, *śādeh* 12:4 and 14:5 (reverse order!).[37]

So let us take another look at 12:4. The only earlier passage that mentions "beast and bird" is 9:9 ("bird and beast," reverse order!), part of the interlude in the supplementary foe cycle. That earlier verse, 9:9, provides the occasion for 12:4. The earlier verse closely followed the verb *bḥn,* "test" (9:6), so that when *bḥn* occurs again (12:3), the prophet is moved to "take up a lamentation for the pastures of the wilderness" (9:9). That is to say, 9:9, following closely on 9:6 *(bḥn),* stimulates the production of 12:4 when 12:3 has *bḥn,* so that in a way 12:4 is the fulfillment of the command of 9:9. Furthermore, the imagery of 12:4 is not really alien to that of the rest of 12:1-6—"grass" (12:4) picks up "plant" and "water" in 12:2, and *ra'at* (12:4) is parallel to *ṭôbôt* (12:6). The verse then offers the link from the father complex to the drought complex, just as the drought complex ends with material that links it to the mother complex. And, as I have already suggested (7, b), the final integrating passage, 20:14-18, by giving echoes of 15:5-9, signals to us that when the man and day complexes were added—and therewith the integrating passage—the drought complex had already been inserted into the corpus.

Question: given the close relation between 14:2-6 and 15:5-9, is it possible that the original form of the drought complex was simply 14:2-6 + 15:5-9, a totality in which Jeremiah describes a drought (14:2-6), gives his reaction (15:5), and records God's explanation (15:6-9)? The evidence of 12:4 and 20:16 might suggest this.

Another question: though the editorial superscription, "about the drought," 14:1, may be late, is the material about the drought *(bṣrt)* here in part because of the *mibṣar/boṣer/maṣôr* word-play that we have traced? Compare 17:8, where *baṣṣoret* does appear in the poetry.

Further, the dialogical nature of the material in the drought complex makes it plausible material to add to the dialogical material of the confessions.

f. The Pride-Glory Collection (13:1-11, 15-27)

There are several units of material in chapter 13 that share vocabulary for "pride" or "glory"; there seems to be no inner unity to this collection (thus, for example, no inclusio at beginning and end)—hence I shall call it a "collection" rather than a complex.

The waistcloth episode (13:1-11), with the word *gā'ôn*, "pride" (13:9), is linked to the end of the father complex, which contained *gā'ôn* (of the Jordan) (12:5). The waistcloth passage also contains the word *tip'eret*, "glory" (13:11). Then we find in vv. 15-17 an oracle with various synonyms for "pride" in all three verses, but specifically *gewâ* in v. 17, etymologically related to *gā'ôn*. There follows then an oracle with *tip'eret* (v. 18 contains the word), which picks up a catchword from vv. 15-17—*tered* (v. 17) and *yarad* (v. 18). Thereafter we find another *tip'eret* oracle (v. 20 contains the word), which meanwhile has picked up more catch-words from v. 17—"eyes" and *'ēder*, "flock," and another from vv. 18-19—*rō'š* (v. 21), parallel with *mar'ašôtêkem* (v. 18) (or whatever the correct text of this word is).[38] The oracle that begins in v. 20

continues through v. 27: *r'h,* "see," appears again in vv. 26 and 27, "skirts are lifted up" appears in both vv. 22 and 26, and "flocks" (v. 20) is associated with "field" (v. 27). Further, one suspects that *śādeh,* "field" (v. 27), helps to link this collection with the drought complex that follows (*śādeh,* 14:5).

g. Further Secondary Material in Chapters 12-16

Let us now work through these chapters to see whether we can discern the basis for the inclusion of various miscellaneous oracles and other units scattered through the collection.

(1) 12:7-17. There seems no good reason to suspect the integrity of the poem in vv. 7-13. It is true that the first-person reference to Yahweh seems to change to the third person in vv. 12-13, but Rudolph (I think rightly) excises "for the sword of Yahweh devours" in v. 12 as an eschatological expansion, and suggests that "the fierce anger of Yahweh" in v. 13 is a fixed phrase, possible in the mouth of Yahweh (for which compare Lam. 2:22).

The poem is an extraordinary one, in which Yahweh himself sings a lament over his beloved people. The poem appears to be linked both to the olive-tree poem in 11:15-16 (*ydd: y*ᵉ*dīdût* 12:7, *lîdîdî* 11:15,[39] *bāśār* 12:12 and 11:15, and to the second half of the father complex, 12:1-6 (enlarged by v. 4) (*'bl* qal 'lament' 12:11 and 12:4[40]); the word "house" (12:7, "my house") is linked to *both* poems (11:15 "my house," 12:6 "house of your father"). We must conclude, then, that 15:7-13 was inserted after 11:1-17 was integrated with 11:18-12:6. The verses that follow, vv. 14-17, are plainly midrashic, here because of *naḥ*ᵃ*lâ* (vv. 7, 8, 9, linked to vv. 14, 15).

(2) 13:12-14. The presence of this passage here is

something of a mystery to me. There is a possible link of *šḥt* hiphil between 13:9 and 14, but this verb is perhaps too common to serve as the specific catchword here. It occurred to me that *motnayim,* "loins," in v. 11 (not a common word in the prophets) suggested a drunkenness passage, because in Isa. 21:3 "my loins" is followed in v. 4 by the verb *tʿh,* "reel," a verb often (though not in that passage) associated with drunkenness; but it may simply be that a late editor had in mind an incident like Noah's drunkenness (Gen. 9:20ff) or perhaps Lot's (Gen. 19:30ff), in which nakedness and drunkenness are associated.

(3) 16:10-15. Verses 10-13 and 14-15 are two units that have obviously been added at a late stage: vv. 10-13 are a catechetical midrash on vv. 1-9 (cf. 9:11-15), and vv. 14-15 a hopeful addition to v. 13.

(4) 16:16-18. These verses, mentioning "fishers," are evidently here for a rather striking reason. The word "fishers" appears three times in the Old Testament: in Ezek. 47:10, which is of course irrelevant to the discussion here; in the present Jeremiah passage; and in Isa. 19:8. It is the Isaiah passage that has triggered the presence of the Jeremiah passage here, for the Isaiah passage says, "The fishers will mourn and lament" ("lament" = *w*^{e}*'āb*^{e}*lû*), and the Jeremiah passage is therefore added to Jer. 16:1-9, which offers *'ēbel* in 16:7. (Admittedly, somewhere nearer Jer. 14:2 might have offered a more plausible place of insertion [14:2 offers both *'āb*^{e}*lâ* and *'uml*^{e}*lû*—Isa. 19:8 has both *'āb*^{e}*lû* and *'umlālû*] but it may be that 14:1-16:9 was perceived as a continuity that was not open to interruption, and/or that 16:1-9 is rich in the vocabulary of lamentation.)[41]

Verses 19-21 are present presumably because of the association between the context of v. 20 and the mention of "idols" in v. 18.

h. A Preliminary Survey of the Material in Chapters 17-20

Chapter 17 contains a curious mélange of material in the first 13 verses. Verses 1-4 make up a passage (of poetry, at least in part) that is evidently linked with the two oracles that follow (vv. 5-8, 9-10) by the catchword "heart"; all of this material (vv. 1-10) seems to be of a wisdom genre. There follow three verses—v. 11 on the partridge and vv. 12-13 on the glorious throne. These 13 verses are followed by a "confessional" passage, vv. 14-18, and this in turn by the prose sermon about the sabbath, vv. 19-27. Chapter 18 begins with a symbolic narrative, of the potter's house, rather similar to that of the waistcloth in 13:1-11; then there follows a difficult passage of poetry about the snows of Lebanon (vv. 13-17) and a verse stating what "they" said about plots against Jeremiah (v. 18); then again a confessional passage (vv. 19-23). Chapter 19 offers us the narrative of the pottery flask, and 20:1-6 the narrative of the mocking change of Pashhur's name (an incident perhaps associated with that of the pottery flask). Then, of course, come the final confessional passages—first vv. 7-13, then the climactic passage that I have already called an "integrating" one, vv. 14-18. This material seems at first even more various than that in chapters 11-16. Can we find our way here?

i. The Man and Day Complexes (17:5-10; 17:14-18, 18:18-23, 20:7-13), Closed by the Integrating Passage of the Confessions (20:14-18)

We recall that the initial stratum of chapters 11-15 proved to be the traditional "confessional" material within those chapters, and by the same token my hypothesis (7, b) suggests that the initial stratum of chapters 17-20 will contain similar confessional material. Let us now examine in more detail some data that will substantiate my model.

There is no disputing the extent of the traditional "confessional" material here—thus 17:14-18 is an obvious unit; 18:18 belongs with 18:19-23 (the cohortative in v. 18 echoes that in 11:19, and *naqšîbâ* in 18:18 is picked up by *haqšîbâ* in 18:19, surely more than a catchword association); and 20:13 belongs with the confessional collection[42] (the phrase *nṣl* hiphil plus *miyyad* in 20:13 echoes 15:21—does this suggest that we have parallel closing utterances before the respective integrating passages, 16:1-9 and 20:14-18?).

But what about the extent of the material that contains 17:5? We note the uncommon adjective *'ānûš*, which appears in 15:18 (the feminine *'ănûšâ*) and then in 17:9 and 16.[43] Because of its use with *yôm* in 17:16 (*wᵉyôm 'ānûš*), I suspect that its occurrence in 17:9 marks a structural datum. Further, 17:9-10 shares "heart" and "fruit" with 17:5-8 ("heart" vv. 5, 9; "fruit" vv. 8, 10) in a symmetrical way that also implies intentional structure rather than the happenstance of catchword association. We may conclude, then, that 17:9-10 belongs with 17:5-8 as the contents of the man complex.

I have already recorded surprise that 17:5-10 should turn out to be part of the initial stratum (7b).

An exegesis of vv. 5-8 suggests that it is a confession after all. The commentators normally take this passage as a wisdom passage similar to Psalm 1, contrasting the shrub in the desert (= the man who trusts in man) with the deep-rooted tree planted near water (= the man who trusts in the Lord), and further assume that Psalm 1 was written after Jer. 17:5-8.[44] But this is to miss the point. The point here is the specific one that the shrub and the deep-rooted tree respond differently *to lack of water:* the desert shrub "does not see good come" (*ṭôb* here may mean "rain"),[45] and bears no fruit, but the tree continues to bear fruit even in a time of drought.

If we look back now at 12:1-2 (see 7d), we see that Jeremiah has offered us two variations on the pattern of Psalm 1, so that it becomes unlikely in the extreme that Psalm 1 was written after Jer. 17:5-8. And if we conclude that Jer. 17:5-8 is a variation on Psalm 1, we may speculate that the hapax *yûbal,* "watercourse" (17:8), is Jeremiah's variation on *yibbôl*, "wither," in Psalm 1:3—the phrase preceding these words is close. Finally, we may note that the pattern of imitating Psalm 1 continues in Ezek. 19:10-14, where the passage refers specifically to Zedekiah's mother.

Now, if Jer. 12:1-2 expressed not a wisdom generality but a personal testimony of Jeremiah's, and if Ezek. 19:10-14 is a personal reference, are we not driven to ask whether Jer. 17:5-8 is not a personal testimony also? And it seems that it is. In 15:18 Jeremiah has suggested that God is like a deceitful brook, like waters that fail, and in 15:19 God suggests that Jeremiah repent and learn again to depend upon God rather than on public approbation. The passage 17:5-8 then *gives the substance of Jeremiah's repentance to God,* and it thus really does belong in the series of "confessions." Jeremiah has been depending on public approbation (15:19); now he says, "cursed is the man who trusts in man" (17:5). No wonder God has seemed to him like a dry stream-bed (15:18): Jeremiah has been like a shrub in the desert that knows no water. Now he is determined to repent and trust in God (17:7), to be a tree with deep enough roots (17:8) so that when the drought comes (17:8) and

God seems absent, seems like waters that fail (15:18), he can still bear fruit in his calling (17:8). This passage, then, reflects Jeremiah's response to God's prescription and emerges as a powerful member of the series of "confessions," offering fresh insight into Jeremiah's perceived relation to God.

If, however, in our pursuit of the initial stratum of material, we work back before 17:5, to 17:1-4, to see whether this material too might be included in the initial stratum, we find that we have gone too far: the material in this passage (whatever may have been its original shape; see 7, k) did not belong to the initial stratum. We can see this from the fact that none of the confessional passages in chapters 17-20 reflect any material here;[46] by the fact that the hope complex in chapters 30-31 begins and ends with *geber* (30:6, 31:22; see chap. 9 [4]); and by the fact that the prophets complex in chapter 23 begins with "heart," *geber,* and *'îš* (23:9; see chapter 9, [2]). These later complexes were so shaped because of the earlier shape of 17:5ff, so far as we can tell. We may conclude, then, that 17:5 does begin the new section of the initial stratum of chapters 17-20.

I must now say a word about the internal organization of the initial stratum in chapters 17-20 and the parallels with the initial stratum of chapters 11-16. We found a well-wrought structure in the initial stratum of chapters 11-15: two pairs of laments and replies, the ends of the first pair and the beginning of the second pair linked together by the words "your father" and "my mother"; and all of this closed by the vocation to celibacy, 16:1-9. The organization of the initial stratum of chapters 17-20 is different: there are five sections—the wisdom meditation (= the man complex, 17:5-10), in which Yahweh is referred to in the third person, though in v. 10 Yahweh replies without being addressed directly; then three confessions, in which Yahweh is addressed in the second person (17:14, 18:19, 20:7); and finally, the summarizing confession, which, with its third-person reference to Yahweh (20:16), balances the wisdom meditation, though of course the emotional tone is at the opposite end of the spectrum. Further, too, the contrast between the wisdom passage and the following three confessions is indicated by the phrases "cursed be the day" and "cursed be the man" in 20:14, 15.

As I have already affirmed,[47] this material can be brought under the rubric of "Jeremiah's intercourse with God." But I register here the obvious fact that these five passages (in 17:5-20:18) do not offer the consistent dialogue between Jeremiah and Yahweh that the confessions of chapters 11-15 did. We have now only hints of dialogue: 17:10 is a kind of answer from Yahweh, but Jeremiah had not addressed him in the first place, and it is more of a meditation on Yahweh's part than a direct answer; and though 18:18 gives the words of Jeremiah's enemies, as do 11:19 and 20:10, yet nothing more is heard from Yahweh, and otherwise it is Jeremiah's words alone that we hear.

I have already reviewed the way in which this material is ordered by means of words for time (see 7, b). But there are other ways in which the initial strata of 17-20 and 11-15 echo each other besides the sharing of *'ĕnôš* and the words for time that I have mentioned. The words *ṭôb(â)* and *ra'â* are likewise shared (11:23; [12:4—the secondary insertion]; 12:6; 15:11 twice, 21; 17:6, 17, 18; 18:20, 23) but are evidently not patterned in a way that helps us discern structure (and, *nota bene,* neither word appears in the integrating passage, 20:14-18). One finds other parallels: the double verb of

17:14 ("heal me, Yahweh, and I shall be healed"), which echoes both the double verb of 11:18 ("Yahweh made it known to me and I knew") and the use of "heal" in 15:18;[48] "my lips" (17:16), which echoes "my mouth" (15:19); *śᵉḥôq,* "sport," 20:7, which echoes *mᵉsaḥᵃqîm* (15:17); *ḥerpâ* (20:8), which echoes 15:15; the cohortative in 20:10, which echoes earlier cohortatives in 11:19 and 18:18; 20:12, which is a doublet of 11:20, but which can hardly be a secondary addition—but all of these are the sort of echoes that one might expect from variations on the same thematic material.

We recall that neither 15:15-21 nor 16:1-9 gives any evidence of echoing the drought complex, but that 12:4, a secondary addition, and 20:16, in the final integrating passage, do echo that material. Now we must ask the question whether there is any further evidence within the initial stratum of chapters 17-20 for the presence of the drought complex at the time when this material was integrated into the Jeremianic corpus. The answer would seem to be positive. We have first the thematic reference to a drought in 17:8. And then in the second "confession" (18:18-23) we have strong echoes of 15:7-8—*šakkūlôt,* "childless", 18:21 and *šikkaltî,* "I have bereaved," 15:7;[49] *'almānôt*, "widows," 18:21 and 15:8.[50] Question: is it significant that echoes of the drought complex (which by now is the *middle* term between the father complex and the mother complex) are found in the *first* unit (the man complex, 15:8), in the *third* unit (18:18-23), and in the *fifth* unit (20:16), skipping the second (17:14-18) and fourth (20:7-13) units?

We need next to inquire about any possible echoes of chapters 2-10 within the initial stratum of chapters 17-20 (we recall that 15:19 offered a quartet on *šwb,* echoing the prelude and postlude in 4:1 and 8:4, and that 16:9 ended with "bride," which may serve to echo 2:2). There do seem to be such echoes, and several of them appear within 17:5-10. (1) If 16:9 ended with a word suggesting 2:2, 17:6 offers a phrase suggesting 2:3: *w*ᵉ*lō yir'eh kî yābô' ṭôb*, "and he shall not see good come," which looks like a parody, both in meaning and in assonance, of *rā'â tābô'* in 2:3 (and its variations in the foe cycle), and this observation is confirmed by the role played by *ṭôb(â)* and *rā'â* in the initial stratum of chapters 17-20. (2) The description of the parched land in 17:6 is modeled closely on 2:6 (*'ereṣ* plus an adjective plus a negative phrase); further, the adjective *'āqôb*, modifying "heart" in 17:9 reminds us of the verb "supplant," punning on the name "Jacob," in 9:3 (*'āqôb ya'qōb*), and the participle *bōḥen*, whose subject is Yahweh, in 17:10, coming soon after *'āqôb*, reminds us of the verb *bḥn*, subject Yahweh, in 9:6. In other words, 17:5-10 offers us (a) an echo of 2:3 (matching the echo of 2:2 in 16:9?), and (b) echoes of both an early verse of the harlotry cycle proper (2:6) and of verses from the supplementary foe cycle (9:3, 6). So just as 17:5-10 seems to offer echoes of the beginning and the end of the drought complex, so now it also seems to offer simultaneously echoes of the beginning and end of chapters 2-10. Dare we conclude that the initial stratum of *chapters 11-16* took shape at the same time as the harlotry cycle and the first foe cycle did, and that the *drought complex* and the initial stratum of *chapters 17-20* were added at roughly the time when the supplementary foe cycle was added? It would seem a likely hypothesis.

Matching these echoes of chapters 2-10 in 17:5-10 are a couple of similar echoes in the integrating confession, 20:14-18 (both of them, as a matter of fact, in 20:16): *t*ᵉ*rû'â* echoes 4:19[51] and *soh*ᵒ*rāyim* echoes 6:4 as well as 15:8.[52]

It now seems plausible that we have at least two stages

of development of this material: (1) the father and mother complexes, completed by the integrating call to celibacy; (2) the addition of the drought complex between the father and mother complexes, and the addition of the man and day complexes; all completed by the integrating confession, 20:14-18.

j. Secondary Material in Chapters 17-20

Now to account for the balance of the material to be found in chapters 17-20.

(1) 17:1-4. This passage will be discussed in 7, k.

(2) 17:11-13. There are two bits of material here: v. 11, on the partridge that steals, and vv. 12-13 on Yahweh enthroned in the temple. One can only surmise that the two are linked by the word *'zb* (*ya'azbennû,* v. 11; *'ozebêkā, 'azebû* v. 13 and that the pair is then inserted here because of the verb *ktb* (*yikkātebû* v. 13), linked with v. 1 (*ketûbâ*).[53]

(3) 17:19-27. The sabbath passage is here because of a double link: it was triggered by *kissē'*, "throne" (vv. 12, 25), and by the three occurrences of *yôm* in vv. 16-18, which offer occasion for the sevenfold repetition of the word in the present passage.

(4) 18:1-12. The key word in this passage on the incident at the potter's house is *nišḥat*, "was spoiled" (18:4), which appears in the book of Jeremiah only otherwise in 13:7, where the waistcloth "was spoiled." I suggest that the present passage appears here, after the confessional material of 17:14-18, because of the position of the waistcloth incident after the first confessional passage 11:18-12:6; there are certainly enough phraseological parallels between 11:18-12:6 and 17:14-18 to have encouraged such an arrangement.

(5) 18:13-17. The presence of this passage here is another instance, and one of the most convincing, of the process of "adjunction by preexisting association." The passage mentions "Lebanon," and is here, directly after the "potter" passage, because it reflects the association of "potter" and "Lebanon" in *adjoining* verses of Isaiah —Isa. 29:16 and 17 respectively. Two things must be said here. First, this passage in Isa. 29 is the only other preexilic passage in the prophets that contains a reference to potter and clay. Second, the two verses in Isaiah of course belong to separate oracles; they adjoin because of the catchword *yeḥašeb* common to both of them—this form is not common, appearing only once otherwise in Isaiah, namely, 32:15, a close variation on 29:17. But it is the juxtaposition, I submit, of "potter" and "Lebanon" that leads to the parallel juxtaposition in Jer. 18.

(6) 19:1-20:6. This is one sustained narrative, according to the commentators. It is assumed that the material is here because of the catchword *potter*[54] from 18:2, 3; but there is a more likely solution (one would have to ask why 19:1 was not inserted *before* 18:18-23 rather than after it!), and again it is a solution based on adjunction by preexisting association. Both 13:1 and 19:1, after the introductory words, begin with *hālôk wᵉqānîtā*, "go and buy." It is likely, then, that 19:1ff was inserted after 18:18-23 because of some likeness between 18:18-23 and 12:1-3, 5-6: I would suggest the phrase *wᵉ'attâ yhwh yāda'tā*—it is so found in 18:23 and 12:3 contains the phrase *wᵉ'attâ yhwh yᵉda'tānî*; these are the only two examples of this shape of phrase in Jeremiah.[55] I suggest that 19:1 was inserted here, after 18:23, because of the association between 12:3 and 13:1.

If 20:1-6 follows on chapter 19, then *māgôr missābîb* here of course anticipates the same phrase in 20:10. It might be assumed that 20:7-18 was the lament uttered by Jeremiah on the occasion of his being imprisoned in the stocks (20:2), in which case the presence of this passage needs no other excuse.[56]

k. Later Insertions That Seem to Carry Larger Structural Functions: 17:1-4 and 11:1-17

Neither of these two passages seems to have been incorporated into the corpus of material because of any thought-association with material just preceding (unless 17:1-4, with "iron," is there because of "iron" in 15:12, but the distance is remote, and the possibility remote as well). Since each comes before a respective half of the primary stratum in chapters 11-20, and because, as we shall see, both of them seem to reflect the "new covenant" passage, 31:31-34, it seems best to deal with them separately, at this point. Let us deal first with 17:1-4.

(1) 17:1-4. This passage is another "heart" saying, prefixed to 17:5-8 + 9-10. Its original text is somewhat in doubt: there are both textual problems and instances of prose expansion, so far as we can tell, but John Bright's reconstruction will do for the purpose of our structural analysis here. Though there may be a light linkage with 15:12 ("iron and bronze," linked to "iron and *šamîr*" there) and thus with the material in 15:10-21, the more obvious links may well be with the "new covenant" passage, 31:31-34, with the use of *ktb*, "sin," "heart," and "tablet" (17:1), as implying the old covenant. The material in the new covenant passage (at least after the first half of 31:33a) is poetic in form, and the parallels of 17:1-4 are with the latter part of that passage.

(2) 11:1-17. This passage is baffling, both in its inner

structure and in its place in the corpus. I have already taken note (7, c) of the obvious fact that 11:1-17 resembles 7:1-8:3 in phraseology; but I must now go on to say that whereas 7:1-8:3 had a kind of inner structure (Chap. 5), it is not at all easy to find structure here. Let me set down what data I can collect and see what conclusions we might draw.

(a) Though there is a general sharing of the Deuteronomistic prose style of 7:1-8:3, there are several phrases and words that are not common coin of that style, which occur here. Aside from the poem in vv. 15-16 (for which see below), we may note the phrase *'ārûr hā'îš 'ᵃšer* (v. 3), which reflects 20:15; the phrase *habbᵉrît hazzō't*,[57] and *qešer*, revolt,[58] which are quite singular.

(b) One wonders whether 11:1-5 is not a kind of Jeremianic echo of Deut. 27:15-26 (note especially vv. 15 and 26 there) or 28:16ff, as Jer. 7:1ff was an echo of Deut. 12:1ff. (Do we have the beginning and the end of Ur-Deuteronomium here?!) The phrase in Jer. 11:5, with *'nh* and *'āmēn* would seem to be thoroughly distinctive.[59]

(c) As far as the inner "structure" is concerned, the expression *habbᵉrît hazzō't* occurs in v. 2 in an introduction, and then in vv. 3 and 8, so that this suggests a kind of inclusio for vv. 3-8. It is possible that the word *bᵉrît* and the associated verb *'ābî'* in v. 8 produce vv. 9-11: v. 10 has *bᵉrîtî*, and v. 11 begins *hinᵉnî mēbî' ᵃlêhem rā'â*; and that this *rā'â* in turn produces v. 12 (*bᵉ'ēt rā'ātām*), which in turn produces v. 14, with the same phrase: v. 13 is no doubt intrusive, on the model of 2:28a, because v. 12 shares with 2:27 "save" and "in their time of trouble."[60] But such "structure" seems very slack.

(d) The poem in vv. 15-16 seems to come on quite

unannounced. I would suggest with some tentativeness that the train of thought is based on 7:16ff. The paragraph in 7:16 begins "do not pray. . ." as does 11:14; the next section of chapter 7 contains *bāśar* (v. 21). Does this pattern trigger the poem in 11:15, which contains the phrase *beśar qodeš*?[61] This suggestion is at least plausible in the light of the other examples of "adjunction by preexisting association" that we have found elsewhere in these chapters of Jeremiah. Then v. 17 would be a reprise, picking up (by *nṭ'*) the tree-image, and by *rā'â* twice picking up earlier occurrences of that word. Verses 16-17 then lead logically into material in the father complex (*nṭ'* 12:2), so that 11:1-17 serves as a kind of preface to the material that begins in 11:18. Indeed, does *bāśar* (v. 15) serve to anticipate the initial stratum of chapters 17-20 (*bāśar,* 17:5) as *nṭ'* (11:17) anticipates the initial stratum of chapters 11-16?

(e) But the basic anticipation of the passage, as with 17:1-4, would seem to be with the new covenant passage: *habberît hazzō't* in 11:17 is parallel to *zō't habberît* in 31:33. The passage 11:1-17 then depicts the call to obey the old covenant, to which the people failed to respond, so that a new covenant becomes necessary.

(3) *Possible Solutions of the Problem of 11:1-17 and 17:1-4*. Either 11:1-17 and 17:1-4 are *not* related in their structural function, or they *are.* (a) If they are not related, then I would suggest that 17:1-4 is a late insertion, linking 15:10-21, 16:1-9 (by "iron and *šāmîr,*" v. 1, echoing "iron and bronze" in 15:12) with 17:5ff (by "heart"), and that 11:1-17 is a preface to the primary stratum of chapters 11-20, plus additional material, ending with the new covenant passage.[62] (b) If they are related—and they may well be, considering the occurrence of "iron [furnace]" in 11:4, parallel then to "iron" in 17:1—then

we may have in 11:1-17 an anticipation of the *first* half of the new covenant passage ("this is the covenant," 31:33a) and in 17:1-4 an anticipation of the *second* half of the new covenant passage ("write it upon their heart," 31:33b); in this case we should have to believe that the two main sections of the primary stratum of chapters 11-20, namely, 11-16 and 17-20, were still perceived as sections (and why not?). But the true state of affairs was perhaps even more complicated than these models would suggest.

8

Additions to the Call (1:15-19)

BEYOND the editorial superscription at the beginning of chapter 1, the call section, as we have seen, consists of the call proper (1:4-10) and two visions, the second of which points ahead as far as the foe cycle. The balance of chapter 1 is either all prose, or else a mixture of prose and poetry: one might discern some poetry within the striking vocabulary of some of the verses. But one wonders whether this material was not added here at a rather late stage in the development of the corpus, to keep pace, so to say, with the addition of chapters 11-20, since the phrasing of 1:15-19 offers reminiscences of material from chapters 11-20. Thus "gates of Jerusalem" (v. 15) reminds one of the sabbath sermon, where that phrase is repeated several times (17:19, 21, 27, cf. 24, 25). The language of v. 16 reminds one of the Temple Sermon. The material in vv. 17-18 is heavy with parallels to the material of chapters 11-20, especially to the confessional material proper. Thus the double use of "dismay" (*ḥtt* niphal) in v. 17 is quite close to the usage of 17:18, and the mention of "bronze wall(s)" (the plural may be wrong) in v. 18 reminds one of 15:20. Further, "gird up your loins" reminds one of the waistcloth passage (13:1-11). Of course this new material has its own links with what has come before in the visions: thus *petaḥ* (v. 15) is linked to *tippātaḥ* (v. 14). It looks very much as if a traditional core of material (like v. 17) was enlarged to continue the kind of rhetorical balance that the growing corpus at the end of the collection seemed to require.

9

Postscript: Remarks on Some of the Collections after Chapter 20

WE have come to the end of my inquiry. Since the core of Jer. 1-20 make up a unity, I need not carry my analysis further now, though if valid, the technique could obviously be extended. But before drawing my conclusions, I would like to make a few observations on the way in which the material beyond chapter 20 fits into the architecture of chapters 1-20.

(1) The Royal House Complex (21:1-23:6). The opening passage in this complex is obviously linked to 20:16 by the word *boqer*—these are the only two occurrences of the word in Jeremiah. Further, Lundbom points out that the complex begins with "Zedekiah" (21:1, 3, etc.) and ends with *yhwh-ṣidqenu* (23:6).[1]

(2) The Prophets Complex (23:9-40). This complex begins with the words *lēb, geber,* and *'îš,* which echo 17:5 and 20:15; and the center-point of the last poem in the

complex, 23:29,[2] offers *k^{e}'ēs* in the context of Yahweh's word, a usage echoing 20:9; it looks then as if this complex as a whole echoes 17:5-20:18.

(3) The Vision of the Figs (24). In form, this passage closely follows that of the two visions in chapter 1 (vv. 11-14). It is a vision that of course came late in the prophet's career. Since the second vision (1:13-14), of the foe from the north, was no doubt more than fulfilled by Nebuchadnezzar's first invasion, this vision was no doubt placed here, after the closing confession (with its reminiscences of 1:4-10), as the fresh and encouraging word for the future.

(4) The Hope Complex (30-31). This collection likewise begins with *geber* (30:6) and ends with it (31:22). This inclusio[3] is reinforced by the symmetry *zākār* (30:6) and *n^{e}qēbâ* (31:22). The collection of material of course repeats many of the themes of earlier material in the book of Jeremiah. Thus in this first oracle (30:5-7) one finds *ša'^{a}lû ûr^{e}'û* (v. 6) parallel with 6:16; the root *yld* (v. 6) parallel with 20:14, and so on; *hayyôm* (v. 7) and *'ēt ṣārâ* with 15:11; the verb *yš'* niphal, "be saved," parallel with 17:14, and perhaps 23:6; then 30:10 continues with "save" and "Jacob," so that the linking words continue. And as indicated, 31:22 seems to close off the collection, but 31:31-34 seems to be an addition, linked to 31:22 by *ḥ^{a}dāšâ*. I have already suggested (7, k [3]) that this "new covenant" passage may close off inclusiones begun by 11:1-17 ("covenant") and 17:1-4 ("written," "tablet," "heart").

(5) The Oracle to Baruch (45). The key word here, *yāgôn*, "sorrow" (v. 3), suggests that this passage was originally directly following the end of chapter 20, which contains the same word (v. 18 there).[4] We saw in my discussion of chapters 12-15 how subsequent additions to

the corpus moved earlier material to a steadily greater distance, so that first 14:1ff were added, then 13:1ff, then 12:7ff. So here; I suspect that chapter 45 was originally added to 20:18, then other complexes were added one by one, each displacing earlier material. The passage then served, as 20:14-18 had, as a further inclusio with 1:4-10, for we note that the four verbs in 45:4 ("build," "break down," "plant," "pluck up") are in a different order from that in 1:10, that one finds *hrs* instead of *nts̩*, and that the verbs serve a different function here: in 1:10 God seems to say, "I must smash, and then I can build," while in 45:4 he seems to say, "I have built, but I must smash."

10

Where Do the Data Lead Us? Evidence for the Urrollen?

a. General Gains

As I seek to draw this mass of detailed work together, let me first specify the general gains achieved.

(1) I have demonstrated, I believe, that there *is* structure to the material, and I have tried to demonstrate just what that structure is. The structure has become apparent by application of techniques of rhetorical criticism, many of which I have had to devise on the spot. I have affirmed that the device of inclusio plays a significant role in larger structures consisting of many oracles, as well as within a single oracle. I have found that "road-maps" at the beginning and at the end of the material, namely, the seed oracle, 2:2-3, and the integrating passages, 16:1-9 and 20:14-18, offer an overall view of the largest structures, and that such "unex-

pected" patterns as the variation of speakers, as well as more "expected" patterns like the symmetry of key words and phrases, or assonance, help to shape smaller structures.

(2) Our exegesis of Jeremiah has been aided at many points. In particular, we have been enabled to gain a better understanding of 9:2,[1] of 15:11-12, and of 17:5-8; we have been able to use the MT for the first two of these passages, and have been reassured as to the order of verses in 11:18-12:6. In particular, the elucidation of who is speaking in a given verse corrects the exegesis of the commentaries, notably in 9:1-2 and 10:23-25.

(3) I have established, in most cases with a high degree of plausibility, the immediate stimulus for the insertion of secondary material at a given point in the growing corpus of material. Often the stimulus is an unusual catchword; on one occasion it seems to be a "catchword that is not there," because we have an *ad hoc* opposite (5:30-31). But just as often, it would seem, the stimulus is a more complex one based upon a preexisting association: either a sequence of thought earlier in the Jeremianic corpus, or a sequence or association of thought in earlier material available to the compiler—in one or two cases from Isaiah. For the sake of convenience, let me list the examples of "adjunction by preexisting association" that I have uncovered or seem to have uncovered:

examples with high likelihood	*examples with fair likelihood*
Jer. 9:22-25 because of 6:10-11	Jer. 16:16-18 because of Isa. 19:8
18:1-12 because of 11:18-13:11	19:1-20:6 because of 12:3 + 13:1
18:13-17 because of Isa. 29:16-17	11:15 because of 17:16-21.

In addition, there are structures on a larger scale that seem to be based upon structural patterns or word-patterns from earlier prophets,[2] specifically: Jer. 1:11-12 may be associated with the harlotry cycle because of the use of *maqqēl* in Hos. 4:12, and the harlotry cycle may be followed by the foe cycle because of the sequence in Hosea, where 5:8ff follow 4:4-5:7 and the vineyard imagery is no doubt to be derived from Isa. 1-5.

It might be worthwhile, then, for commentators to look for evidence for adjunction by preexisting association in other prophetic material. For example, in Isa. 5:18 we have *habl̂ê haššāw'*, "cords of falsehood," after a description of Sheol in v. 14; is this because Psalm 18:6 (= II Sam. 22:6) has the phrase *heblê še'ôl*, "cords of Sheol"?

b. Evidence for the Urrollen?

Now that the first question (is there structure?) has been answered with a fair degree of certainty, we are pressed to a second question: who is responsible for the structure here found? The fact that this second question is separate from the first, and far from answerable with the same certainty, does not preclude its being raised.

There can be no certainty as to what Jeremiah could do, or could not do, or as to what Baruch or some subsequent editor could do, or could not do. But three things seem clear.

(1) Jeremiah (like Isaiah before him, and Deutero-Isaiah after him) was exceedingly skillful in his use of assonance.[3] To pick out a small example out of dozens: in 15:6 we have *'att* followed by a word with *ṭ* *(nāṭaštā)*, and in the next line *wā'aṭ* (pronounced *wā'aṭṭ*), followed

by a word with *t* (*'et-*). This kind of thing Jeremiah seems to have done effortlessly; one can spend many happy hours chasing such delights through his lines (and the lines of other Old Testament poets as well).

(2) The typical techniques for secondary insertion of material seem to be either that of catchwords or that of adjunction by preexisting association (see 10, a [3]).

(3) But the large-scale structures that I have uncovered seem often to be manifested by means of assonance: the linking of *qārôb* and *rāḥôq* in 12:2 with *yiqqā-berû* and *yiqqāre*^{a}*h* in 16:6 (7, b) is a striking example, but we have seen many others: *hammibṣār* (4:5, 8:14) and *bammāṣôr* (10:17), even if one hesitates to accept my suggested vocalization of *mibbōṣer* in 6:27 (4, n) or the possibility of a connection of these with further *ṣ-r* words in 15:11, 17:8, and 20:16 (7, b).

This being the case, the most likely conclusion is that *Jeremiah himself,* at some point in the shaping of these individual poems, saw them in *relation* to each other and used them in the building up of larger structures.

If this conclusion is sound, and it seems altogether likely that it is, then it raises questions that will seem very awkward to some. We had assumed that the unit of utterance in a given instance was the oracle, confined to a few verses. Are we to maintain this assumption in Jeremiah's case and conclude that the symmetries between given oracles arose in the process of their *separate* birth, or are we to abandon the assumption in Jeremiah's case and conclude that his public utterances covered far more material at a time than we are accustomed to imagine? I do not know, and I cannot imagine a methodology at this point that would solve the problem of the process by which the structures came to be: nothing analogous to Beethoven's notebooks are likely to come to light in Jeremiah's case!

But one problem may be brought nearer to solution by these investigations, and that is the perennial issue of Jeremiah scholarship, the identification of the contents of the *Urrolle*; so let us go back once more over some of the conclusions which we have reached in the course of this study.

There is a real contrast between chapters 1-10 and chapters 11-20 in the degree to which an initial stratum has been enlarged by secondary material: we found that except for additions in chapter 3, the Temple Sermon material, and the oracle on idols (10:1-6), most of the text of chapters 1-10 is integrated into a coherent whole. (I had always wondered why I could find no catchwords in chapters 5, 6, and 8; the answer, of course, is that there are none.) By contrast, chapters 11-20 has a skeleton of an initial stratum, but a most complicated tissue of additions. Further, we have seen that the initial stratum of chapters 1-10 can stand rhetorically alone; it does not need the initial stratum of chapters 11-20 for rhetorical completeness (*i.e.*, the seed oracle gives the map, and the call in chapter 1 is a kind of prelude linked by *na'ar*).

Are we in a position now to try to solve the old puzzle of the identity of the scrolls (for there were two) that Jeremiah dictated to Baruch? It might seem foolhardy, when so many other attempts have been made to solve the puzzle in the past, but I submit there is strong evidence before us that we are within reach of a solution. Though the narrative in Jer. 36 is well known, let us look at two details of the chapter. First, the contents of the first scroll: it contained "all the words that I have spoken to you against [or, concerning][4] Israel and Judah and all the nations. . . . It may be that the house of Judah will hear all the evil which I intend to do to them, so that every one may turn from his evil way. . ." (vv.

2-3). Now, whatever may be our detailed judgments about this text ("Jerusalem" instead of "Israel" in v. 2?),[5] it is plain that the initial stratum of chapters 11-20 do not qualify, but that the material of the harlotry and foe cycles do.

Second, the contents of the second scroll: "Then Jeremiah took another scroll," we read, "and gave it to Baruch the scribe. . .who wrote on it at the dictation of Jeremiah all the words of the scroll which Jehoiakim king of Judah had burned in the fire; *wᵉʿôd nôsap ʿălêhem dᵉbarîm rabbîm kāhēmmā*—and then many sayings similar to these were added to them" (v. 32). If this narrative is accurate—and there is no reason to doubt it—then it fits extraordinarily well the structure I have laid bare for chapters 1-10. My suggestion is clear:

first scroll:	the call the harlotry cycle the foe cycle
second scroll:	the same, with the addition of the supplementary foe cycle.

We recall: the first foe cycle was rounded off and complete, with seven sections and a postlude, while the supplementary foe cycle enlarged upon the pattern with three more sections and a coda.

In any event, this suggestion of the identity of the scrolls would seem to be as plausible as any others that have been set forth.[6] And whether we can find certainty in the matter of the identity of the scrolls or not, it would seem that the Jeremianic corpus leads not only theologically in the direction of both Job and Deutero-Isaiah, but rhetorically toward them too, in preparing us for larger rhetorical creations.

Notes

NOTES TO INTRODUCTION

1. Cf. the remarks of J. Philip Hyatt in the *Interpreter's Bible,* 5: 787.

2. Sigmund Mowinckel, *Zur Komposition des Buches Jeremia* (Kristiania: 1914).

3. Cf. here Wilhelm Rudolph, *Jeremia*, 1958 ed., pp. xvii-xviii; 1968 ed., pp. xviii-xix.

4. Otto Eissfeldt, *The Old Testament, An Introduction* (Oxford: Basil Blackwell, 1965), pp. 350-54.

5. See, *e.g.*, John Bright, *Jeremiah*, Anchor Bible (New York: Doubleday, 1965), p. lxi, and note 9 there.

6. *Das Problem der Urrolle* (Gütersloh: Gütersloher Verlagshaus, Gerd Mohn, 1966).

7. Cf. my review of Rietzschel in *Vetus Testamentum* 18 (1968): 400-405. For a more systematic survey of various views on the contents of the scroll, see chap. 10, b below.

8. Bright, p. lvi.

9. Bright, p. lx.

10. Cf. R. B. Y. Scott, Introduction to Isaiah 1-39 in *Interpreter's Bible*, 5: 158.

11. For a good description of what this implies, see James Muilenburg, "Baruch the Scribe," in John I. Durham and J. Roy Porter, eds., *Proclamation and Presence, Old Testament Essays in Honour of Gwynne Henton Davies* (Richmond, Va.: John Knox Press, 1970), pp. 215-38.

12. Much has been written recently about inclusio; the most accessible

treatments are perhaps in M. Dahood's *Psalms I, II, III, Anchor Bible* (New York: Doubleday, 1966-70): see "inclusio(n)" in the index of each of the volumes. I am indebted to Dr. Jack R. Lundbom for pointing out this example to me. See below, nn 16 and 18.

13. They are published in the *Congress Volume, Supplements to Vetus Testamentum* 22 (Leiden: E. J. Brill, 1972).

14. These articles are found in the *Congress Volume* cited in n 13, pp. 88-112, 113-28, and 129-42 respectively.

15. Weiss's essay deals in part with a structural comparison of Ps. 1 and Jer. 17:5-8.

16. Jack R. Lundbom, *Jeremiah: A Study in Ancient Hebrew Rhetoric* (Society of Biblical Literature and Scholars' Press, 1975).

17. See, for example, Albert B. Lord, *The Singer of Tales, Harvard Studies in Comparative Literature* 24 (1960, reprinted by Atheneum Press, 1965).

18. Jack R. Lundbom, *Jeremiah: A Study in Ancient Hebrew Rhetoric*, p. 29; pp. 28-30 deal with the collection.

19. See James Muilenburg, "Form Criticism and Beyond," *Journal of Biblical Literature* 88 (1969): 1-18, as well as some of the bibliography cited by David Noel Freedman in the *Prolegomenon* to G. B. Gray, *The Forms of Hebrew Poetry* (New York: Ktav, 1972), p. li.

20. *VT* 20 (1970): 160-61.

NOTES TO CHAPTER 1

1. The word *na'ar* appears in Jer. again only in 51:22; for the distribution of *n*^{e}*'ûrîm* and *n*^{e}*'ûrôt*, see chap. 2, n 4.

2. I do not take account of occurrences in 3:6-8, since this is no doubt secondary material.

3. For another possible rhetorical link between material in Jer. and in Hos., see 4p.

NOTES TO CHAPTER 2

1. See 4b.

2. The verb *škḥ* does not appear again in Jer. until 13:25.

3. And in v. 25, in what is evidently a gloss; see below.

4. The word *n*^{e}*'ûrîm* appears otherwise in Jer. in 22:21, 31:19, 48:11; as I noted above (chap. 1, n 1), the word *na'ar*, beyond its appearance in 1:6, 7, appears in Jer. only in 51:22; the word *n*^{e}*'ûrôt*, identical in meaning with *n*^{e}*'ûrîm*, is found in Jer. only in 32:30.

5. The identical phrase is also found in 7:34, in a prose section (see below, chap. 5) and the word *kallâ* also appears in Jer. 25:10 and 33:11.

6. With *b*^{e}, the phrase is found otherwise in Jer. only in 5:19 and 15:14; without *b*^{e}, in 6:8, 17:6, and 51:43.

NOTES TO CHAPTER 3

1. Other factors, of course, also shaped the wording of vv. 5-8: one suspects that Isa. 30:6-7 was a model ("land of trouble and anguish," "cannot profit," "empty").

2. In Jer. 4:7 "lion" refers to the foe from the north.

3. These are the only two occurrences of this hiphil participle in Jer.

4. The root *ṭm'* is found otherwise in Jer. only in 7:30, 19:13, and 32:34.

5. *VT* 11 (1961): 170-76.

6. Against Rudolph, who analyzes the grouping of verses to be 20-28 and 29-37.

7. I have access only to an English translation of his work: Heinrich Ewald, *Commentary on the Prophets of the Old Testament,* trans. J. Frederick Smith (London: Williams & Norgate, 1875-80), 3: 102, where his rendering, "and as many as the streets of Jerusalem they sacrificed to Baal," clearly presupposes the Hebrew reflected later in Cornill, Condamin, and Rudolph in *BHS* (see n 8): *ûmispar ḥuṣôt yᵉrūšālaim qiṭṭᵉrû labba'al.*

8. C. H. Cornill, *Das Buch Jeremia* (Leipzig: Tauchnitz, 1905), Condamin, and Rudolph in *BHS* follow the reconstruction assumed for Ewald in n7. Volz and, curiously enough, Rudolph in his commentary, offer *mizbᵉḥôt* instead of *qiṭṭᵉrû*, but this is simply to take over the prosaicized phrasing of 11:13; cf. my study in *JBL* 79 (1960): 351-67. The Greek *ethyon* clearly demands the verb *qiṭṭᵉrû*. See also the evidence from 18:15 below.

9. *JBL* 85 (1966): 419-20, 423-24, 432-33, on Jer. 16:1-9 and 23:1-4.

10. Thus Bright offers the material in the order 3:1-5, 19-25, 4:1-4, and 3:6-18; Rudolph, while presenting the material in the order of the MT, insists: "3_{19}ff. schliesst weder an 3_{14-18} noch (Duhm) an 3_{12}f. an, . . . sondern ist Fortsetzung von 3_{1-5}, wie heute die meisten Exegeten mit Recht annehmen . . ." (1958 ed., p. 27; 1968 ed., p. 29).

11. Beyond the standard ones, see in particular James Muilenburg, "A Study of Hebrew Rhetoric: Repetition and Style," in *Supplements to Vetus Testamentum* 1 (Leiden: E. J. Brill, 1953), pp. 104-5.

12. Though I believe he is wrong to emend *habbōšet 'ākᵉlâ* to *habba'al 'ākal*; the word *habbōšet* is in balance with *bᵉbāšᵉtēnû* in v. 25, as Bright rightly points out. The MT of Jeremiah is perfectly capable of writing *habba'al* (so 2:8, 23) if it is intended. Of course *habbōšet* in v. 24 is a euphemism for Baal, but Jeremiah intends the euphemism. See further below, under section (e), regarding the balance of this word with the verb *b'l* in 3:14a.

13. See the commentators.

14. It is perhaps worth noting that Edward Lane recorded the report that *'abū-l-mar'ati* means "the woman's husband" in certain dialects of classical Arabic (Edward W. Lane, *Arabic-English Lexicon,* 1, Part 1 [London, 1863]: 11, col. 3). Whether the two presumed usages are related or are simply parallel developments from analogous social patterns would of course be difficult to say.

15. Ezekiel solved the tension between the imagery of father and of husband by making God both foster-father and husband to Israel (Ezek. 16).

16. Lundbom (see Intro., n16 above), pp. 37-38.

17. The next occurrence of this noun is in 4:11.

18. This is the first occurrence of the qal verb in the book of Jer. One has *m^e^sûbôtayik* in 2:19 and the hiphil verb in 2:24, but these seem to play no part in the structural pattern of the cycle.

19. The word *'ēk (w^e'ēk, 'ēkâ)* is not common in Jeremiah; it appears (without *'mr*) in 2:21, in local symmetry with the occurrence in 2:23; it does not occur again until 8:8, there again with *'mr,* and in a way that indicates a structural cue; see the discussion in 4, o.

NOTES TO CHAPTER 4

1. See above, 3,b.

2. The only analogous multiple use of verbal forms of *šwb* is to be found in 15:19, which evidently represents a further inclusio; see below, 7, d.

3. The only other collocation of these phrases in Jer. is in three prose passages, 12:16, 38:16, 44:26.

4. There are no other parallels for *ḥzq* plus *mē'^a^nû lāšûb* in Jer.

5. See 6, e.

6. There are no other occurrences of *l^e^yhwh* until the Temple Sermon in Jer. 7.

7. And, within the book of Jer., otherwise in 23:17 and in a prose note in 51:60.

8. And, with other objects, and beyond Jer. 20, 31:8 (a reversal of 4:6), 45:5 (in Baruch's postscript), and 49:5.

9. In the latter part of the book, in 35:17, and twice more without *hinnēh:* 42:17, and 51:64, which imitates 42:17. One also finds it, with other objects, in 32:42 (obj. "all the good"), and 39:16 Qr (obj. "my words"), and with finite hiphil verbs in 32:42, 36:21, and 44:2.

10. And in poetry elsewhere, 49:37, part of an oracle over Elam.

11. In poetry elsewhere in the book of Jer., with the participle *yôṣē't* and subject *rā'â,* in a poetic fragment in 25:32.

12. Compare the discussion in John Gray, *I & II Kings, A Commentary,* 2nd ed. (Philadelphia: Westminster, 1970), pp. 337-38.

13. Compare here Moshe Weinfeld, *Deuteronomy and the Deuteronomic School* (London: Oxford University Press, 1972), pp. 132, 352. The data: 2 Kings 21:12, 22:16 = 2 Chron. 34:24, 2 Kings 22:20 = 2 Chron. 32:28. The phrase also occurs with hiphil forms other than the participle, but in each case the context implies the editorial diction of the Deuteronomic historian, or else later material: 2 Sam. 17:14, 1 Kings 9:9 = 2 Chron. 7:22, 1 Kings 21:21, 21:29 twice; Dan. 9:12, Neh. 13:18.

14. Cf. the earlier occurrence of the verb in 3:24, where the "Shame" (= Baal) has devoured Israel's substance.

15. That is to say, I recorded all occurrences of *dagesh forte* and all presumed occurrences of doubled gutturals and *rēš*: *e.g.*, in 4:5 I recorded *haggidû*, *ba''ārs*, *hi''ās^epû*, *'arrê*, and *hammibṣār*; for a defense of geminated gutturals and *rēš* in Jeremiah's day, see Zellig Harris, "Linguistic Structure of Hebrew, *Journal of the American Oriental Society* 61 (1941): 145, #17. I omitted from the count such rubric-phrases as *n^e'um-yhwh* and (*lākēn*) *kōh 'āmar yhwh* (*'^elōhê yiśrā'ēl*).

16. At the time I made the count, I assumed that v. 27 was a secondary insertion. Whether one counts it or not, the statistical analysis hardly varies. See further below, n30.

17. The identity of this verb is a problem: Rudolph makes the situation plain. The Qr is *yṣt* niphal, "are burned;" the Kt is either a 3rd singular feminine (possible with a plural subject) or an archaic 3rd *plural* feminine of either *yṣt* or *nṣh*, "be devastated." Given the fact that similar phraseology in 4:7 has *nṣh*, and 4:26 has *ntṣ* niphal, "be demolished" (see below, 4g, under point 2), I would opt for the third assonantal variation *yṣt* here in 2:15, and would hence read in Qr.

18. See Hans Wildberger, *Jesaja 1-12 (Biblischer Kommentar, Altes Testament)*.

19. So also Rudolph.

20. Of the standard commentators, only Duhm understands vv. 10-17 to be a single poem. Condamin begins a poem at v. 10, but understands vv. 10-14 and vv. 15-18 to be two poems. Bright does similarly, seeing fragments of poems in vv. 10-17. But Giesebrecht, Volz, Rudolph, Weiser, and Hyatt all begin this section at a different point (Giesebrecht, vv. 7-14, 15-17; Volz and Hyatt, vv. 1-14, 15-17; Rudolph and Weiser, vv. 7-11, 12-17).

21. It would serve no useful purpose here to set out in detail the whole process by which I came to choose the principles of structure at which I finally arrived. Essentially I embarked upon a process of laying in parallel columns material that was parallel in theme or diction. Thus it is plain that 6:1-5 mimics 4:5-7, but then 6:5-11 seems to mimic 5:6-14, while at the same time 5:15-17 is mimicked by 6:22-23. Accounting for the long gaps of unparalleled material between 4:7 and 5:5, and between 6:12 and 21, becomes a necessity. But the charting of the patterns of imperatives was a turning point in my uncovering of structure.

22. See his critical notes in Rudolf Kittel, *Biblia Hebraica*, 3rd ed. (Stuttgart: Privilegierte Württembergische Bibelanstalt, 1931).

23. In the 1st ed. of his commentary (1947). Duhm and Biesebrecht omit the phrase altogether.

24. For the justification for taking vv. 19-22 as one unit, and for the assignment of speakers, see the detailed discussion below, 4g.

25. See recently J. W. McKay, "Man's love for God in Deuteronomy and the father/teacher = son/pupil relationship," *VT* 22 (1972): 426-35.

26. Compare my suggestions about Jeremiah and Moses in *JBL* 83 (1964): 153-64, and 85 (1966): 17-27.

27. The phrase is analogous to 2 Sam. 24:2, *šûṭ-nā' bᵉkol-šibṭê-yiśrā'ēl*: David commands his officers to "go through the tribes of Israel (and number them)."

28. See chap. 3, n9 above.

29. See Berridge, *Prophet, People, and Word of Yahweh*, p. 88.

30. I am uncertain whether v. 27 as a whole is a later insertion or whether the second colon is a gloss (Hyatt, following Peake), or whether v. 27 in general belongs with v. 28, and *lō'* in v. 27 is a mitigating gloss (with most commentators). Rudolph emends to *lāh*. J. Alberto Soggin, *Biblica* (1965), pp. 56-59, thinks that the word is really the *lamed emphaticum* here. For the purpose of the present analysis, a solution of the problem of v. 27 is unnecessary. But see n37 below.

31. So Rudolph on 4:6 (his commentary, 2nd ed. [1958], p. 28; 3rd ed. [1968], p. 32), where he cites Wildberger as well.

32. So Abraham Heschel, *The Prophets* (New York: Harper, 1962), p. 111, on 6:26; he cites midrashic commentators of the second and third centuries as well.

33. The conjunction *kî* may introduce direct discourse (see Gesenius-Kautzsch, *Hebrew Grammar*, 157b); the usage in Gen. 4:23 corresponds nicely with the use suggested here; cf. E. A. Speiser, *Genesis* (*The Anchor Bible*) (New York: Doubleday, 1964).

34. R. E. Wolfe, in the exegesis to Micah in the *Interpr. B.*, 6: 905-6, cites earlier commentators who believe Mic. 1:7 to be a later insertion, a diatribe against idolatry, in which case the verbal resemblance between Mic. 1:7 (*šᵉmāmâ*) and Jer. 4:7 (*šammâ*) may not be relevant; but more recently, Otto Eissfeldt assumes the verse to be original (*The Old Testament, An Introduction* [Oxford: Blackwell, 1965], p. 409.

35. See above, in the paragraph just preceding the material associated with n29.

36. See n17 above.

37. Does the parallel of phraseology here, with *'al-zō't*, reinforce the suspicion that v. 27 is intrusive? See n30 above.

38. So also Rudolph. Berridge, *Prophet, People, and Word of Yahweh*, p. 112, nn217 and 218, agrees, and gives the following evidence: the phrase *bat-'ammî* is used in Jeremiah's speeches, besides this verse, in 8:19, 21, 22, 23, and 14:17—only once, evidently, of a speech of Yahweh's—9:6.

39. So also Volz and Rudolph. Note also that here *kî pit'ōm* could be translated "how suddenly"; see W. F. Albright, in *Mélanges bibliques rédigés en l'honneur d'André Robert* (Paris: Bloud & Gay, 1957), 24-26, for the archaic use of *kî* = "how" in Gen. 1, and Mitchell Dahood, *Psalms III (The Anchor Bible)* (New York: Doubleday, 1970), pp. 405-6, for a similar meaning in various Psalms passages.

40. See above, in the material associated with n23.

41. And perhaps v. 28, if v. 27 is secondary.

42. Compare the data on *lᵉyhwh* given above in the material associated with n6.

43. J. Alberto Soggin suggests an "emphatic *'al*" in the study cited above, n30; Lundbom (see Intro. n28 above), p. 40, suggests an "asseverative" *'al*, following Ugaritic usage, and cites C. Gordon, *Ugaritic Textbook* (Rome: Pontifical Biblical Institute, 1965), entry #162, and M. Dahood, *Biblica* 44 (1963): 293-94.

44. So also Rudolph.

45. But see the remarks below, 4, n, on the last four verses of the cycle (6:27-30).

46. See above, 4, g.

47. *VT* 15 (1965): 111-13.

48. For a complete listing of examples of this phenomenon, see below, 10a(3).

49. Rudolph reads identically except for a third-person verb, thus, "Has the daughter of Zion become. . .?"

50. So Rudolph, Weiser, Hyatt, Bright.

51. Volz: *wā'ōmar;* Rudolph: *'āmartî.*

52. The only other occurrence in Jer. is in 15:9.

53. G. R. Driver's suggestion has been picked up by some other scholars: that we read *mibṣārô tēda'*, "its testing thou knowest," with an Aramaizing infinitive form from the Hebrew *bṣr* = Arabic *bṣr* IV, "observe" (*Journal of Theological Studies* (1955), p. 85; so also Alberto Soggin, *VT* 9 (1959): 95f., and Alfred Guillaume, *PEQ* [1962], pp. 131f). But my own suggestion seems less forced.

54. *E.g.*, Hos. 6:6: "I desire the knowledge of God rather than sacrifices" (*da'at 'ᵉlōhîm mē'ōlôt*); Hab. 2:16, "You will be sated with contempt rather than glory" (*qālôn mikkābôd*).

55. I used 6:22-26 to help clarify the identity of the speakers in the three battle scenes of 4:5-31; see 4, g.

56. See above, 4, a.

57. See above, 4, a.

58. See above, 3, a.

59. There are no other occurrences of *hᵃ-, 'im-, maddûᵃ'* until 8:19, when again this pattern will be a key to the structure. The only other parallel for "how can you say" in Jer. is 48:14.

60. There are no other parallels in Jer. for the pattern *ḥᵃkāmîm* with subject pronoun.

61. Against Rudolph.

62. *Svensk Exegetisk Årsbok* 31 (1966): 21-63 *passim*, esp. pp. 58, 60-62.

63. *Ibid.*, pp. 30, 34-35; for harlotry, see specifically Hos. 4:10, 12, 13, 14, 5:3.

64. The only other passages are Jer. 51:27 and Joel 2:1, 15, all of which are no doubt later.

65. Incidentally, if this is so, it would suggest that the understanding of Hos. 5:8ff (in Jeremiah's generation, at least) was not that of a summons to cultic renewal as Edwin Good suggests was Hosea's original intention (pp. 36ff), but to a battle emergency (most commentators).

66. The only other relevant parallel is Jer. 46:19, *lešammâ tihyeh*.

67. As well as in Isa. 6:11.

68. There is no doubt much *verbal* imitation in the poems of Jeremiah of phraseology from Isaiah and other earlier sources: *e.g.*, Jer. 2:12 *šommû šāmayim*, parallel with Isa. 1:2 *šim'û šāmayim*, but that is another story.

NOTES TO CHAPTER 5

1. Unless the phrase in which it here appears is secondary—so Rudolph; Bright says it "may be" an insertion.

2. The use of *hammāqôm* in Jer. 7:3, 7 of course reflects the repetition of *hammāqôm* (ten times) in Deut. 12.

3. The only other imperatives of *'md* in Jer. are 26:2 and 48:19.

4. Cf. Thomas W. Overholt, *The Threat of Falsehood, SBT,* 2d ser. (London: SCM Press, 1970), p. 11.

5. Condamin also sees it as a separate unit.

6. Cf. n2 above.

7. So Weiser, against Rudolph.

NOTES TO CHAPTER 6

1. Jer. 9:9-10 contain two more parallels to the first foe cycle, but these serve a different function, as we shall see (6,c), and are not included here.

2. See my study of this passage in *VT* 12 (1962): 494-98.

3. The third occurrence, 4:14, carries a metaphorical meaning.

4. May I be allowed a plea here to take the MT seriously when it can be made to yield sense? Not only have the commentators emended v. 2b unnecessarily, but they have followed the LXX in v. 2a and so misunderstood it. The MT text may be translated:

They bend their tongue,
  their bow is a lie,
And not for truth
  are they strong in the land.

The tongue is an *arrow* shot out by the bow of falsehood, a far stronger image than the assumed one of the tongue as a bow that shoots out words. And, one may add, the image of the tongue as an arrow is the same as that of v. 7, where the tongue is specifically called an arrow.

5. Or anywhere else in Jer.

6. The only early occurrence is in 3:21; the verb does not occur again until 13:17.

7. The phrase occurs in Jer. 49:33 and 51:37, and outside of Jer. only in Ps. 44:20.

8. See above, 6, a.

9. See Lundbom (compare Intro., n18 above), p. 81.

10. Volz hints at a connection with "Canaan" here, but I find no commentator who suggests a parallel with the Hosea passage.

11. There are only two other occurrences of *'ôy* plus *lî* in Jer., namely, 15:10 and 45:3 (the latter offering *'ôy-nā' lî*).

12. So Rudolph, Weiser, Bright.

13. So also Berridge, *Prophet, People, and the Word of Yahweh,* p. 194, 56.

14. The resemblance is pointed out by Gerhard von Rad, *Wisdom in Israel* (New York: Abingdon, 1972), chap. 6, n2.

15. See my study in *JBL* 91 (1972): 305-20.

16. For all these, see above 4, a.

17. For another example within Jer. of what I have called "balance by allusion" (Jer. 4:23, 25 in reference to Gen. 1 and 2 respectively), see *JBL* 85 (1966): 409.

18. See above, 4, a.

19. The only occurrences of the qal perfect first singular of *yd'* in Jer. 1-10 are 1:5, 6, 10:23.

20. See chapter 7 below.

21. For this parallel I am indebted to Prof. David Noel Freedman.

22. For a further remark on this patterning, see below, 10, b.

23. The verb appears in Jer. otherwise only in 42:22.

24. These are the only two occurrences of *'ôlāl* in Jer.

25. The only other occurrence of *'ārēl/'orlâ* in Jer. is in 4:4.

26. See above, 4, k.

27. Though the passage is almost universally denied to Jeremiah, Thomas W. Overholt has defended its authenticity, *Journal of Theological Studies* (Apr. 1965), pp. 1-12.

28. The only earlier occurrences of the root are the piel in 2:33 and *limmud* in 2:24.

NOTES TO CHAPTER 7

1. See 6, e.

2. See below, 7, c.

3. There are indirect references to Jeremiah's birth in 1:5, and, of course, the name of Jeremiah's father in the editorial superscription, 1:1.

4. *JBL* 85 (1966): 412-20.

5. These are the only two instances of the participle *bārûk* in the book of Jer.

6. The seeming parallel with *bayyôm hahû'* and *bā'ēt hahî'* in 4:9, 11 is perhaps only fortuitous; see above, 4, f.

7. Volz, Rudolph, Hyatt, and Bright all rearrange the passage in various ways; *e.g.*, Bright wants to reverse the order of 11:18-23 and 12:1-6.

8. I know of no scholar who labels 17:5-8 a confession, but John Skinner (*Prophecy and Religion* [Cambridge: Cambridge University Press, 1922], p. 201, n1) and Hyatt (*Interpr. Bible* 5: 782) list 17:9-10 as a confession.

9. The word *ṣoh^e^rayim* appears otherwise in Jer. only in 6:4.

10. Cf. Hyatt's remarks on both passages.

11. Intro., n12, above, has indicated that Dr. Jack Lundbom first pointed out this inclusio to me.

12. Berridge, *Prophet, People, and the Word of Yahweh,* p. 45, discusses this suggestion and gives literature there in his n110.

13. See above, 3, b.

14. See chap. 6, n11 above, and the accompanying text.

15. And not otherwise in Jer.

16. The only other occurrence of *zkr* in the material that we have been studying is a niphal in 11:19—"that his name be remembered no more," an occurrence that may play a part in the structural symmetry of this material.

17. There are other parallels that seem to have no particular structural significance: Jeremiah's question in 15:18 ("like waters that fail") recalls 2:13, and the "fortified wall" recalls the "fortified cities" of 4:5 and 8:14.

18. So Lundbom (see Intro., n18 above), pp. 100-101.

19. Perhaps some other form of *r'h* is correct here; see BHS.

20. For a further discussion of the imagery of vv. 5-6, see the discussion of 15:11-12 below.

21. The noun otherwise in Jer.: 20:12 (a doublet of 11:20), 25:31, 50:34, 51:36; the verb otherwise in Jer.: 2:9, 29, 50:34, 51:36.

22. So Volz, Condamin, Rudolph, Weiser, Bright, Revised Standard Version, Jerusalem Bible; the New English Bible assigns vv. 11-12 to Yahweh, though not quite with the translation I propose.

23. Volz, Condamin, Rudolph, Weiser, Bright.

24. There is a brief discussion of "running" as a characteristic of the prophets, by O. Bauernfeind under *trechō* in R. Kittel, ed., *TWNT* (Eng. ed. Grand Rapids, Mich.: Wm. B. Eerdmans, 1964-1974), 8: 229-30.

25. This suggestion I owe to my student Mr. Ronald M. Patterson.

26. So 6:14, *lēmōr šālôm šālôm*; 23:25, *lēmōr ḥālamtî ḥālamtî*.

27. *E.g., yômām wālaylâ* separated in Ps. 22:3; see *Psalms III (The Anchor Bible* (New York: Doubleday, 1970), pp. 413-14.

28. So all the commentators.

29. Chap. 6, n4.

30. There is much secondary literature on this section, which has attracted a great deal of interest from the form-critical point of view; a convenient bibliography will be found in Martin Kessler, "From Drought to Exile, A Morphological Study of Jer. 14:1-15:4," in *Proceedings of the Society of Biblical Literature* (1972), pp. 501-25.

31. C. H. Cornill, *Das Buch Jeremia* (Leipzig, 1905), p. 181; Henning Graf Reventlow, *Liturgie und prophetisches Ich bei Jeremia* (Gütersloh: Gütersloher Verlagshaus, Gerd Mohn, 1963), pp. 181-87.

32. But see Kessler, p. 503 and *passim,* for a slightly different view.

33. So Mitchell Dahood, *Biblica* (1967), p. 109.

34. These are the only occurrences of this verb in Jer.

35. Outside the Sabbath Sermon, 17:19-27, and the phrase "those entering by these gates" (7:2, 17:20, 22:2), the only other occurrences of the plural *šᵉʿārîm* in Jer. are 1:15, 22:4, 19, and 51:58.

36. There is uncertainty among the commentators as to the text of "mother of a young man" in 15:8: Volz and Rudolph emend, but Bright simply omits *lāhem* there with the LXX to give grammatical sense, leaving the word *ʾēm* intact. The chance of linkage here is so strong that I would suggest that it would reinforce our conviction that *ʾēm* belongs in the text; "widows" certainly offers a good parallel.

37. Kessler, p. 524, also notices the links with 12:4.

38. Weiser emends to *mērāʾšêkem*, but Dahood saves the consonants, vocalizing *mērāʾšôtêkem*; see *Catholic Biblical Quarterly* 23 (1961): 462. Rudolph favors the first suggestion, but acknowledges the second; see the 1968 ed. of his commentary, and the critical apparatus to BHS.

39. The root *ydd* does not otherwise appear in the book of Jer.

40. In Jer. otherwise only in 4:28, 14:2, 23:10; but the nouns elsewhere, *e.g.*, 16:7.

41. If the association of this passage with Isa. 19:8 is valid, then it gives indirect evidence that Isa. 19:8 was citable prophetic lore at the time when Jer. 16:16-18 came into the collection. Commentators have tended to assign Isa. 19:5-10 to a period later than that for vv. 1-4 and 11-15, which are presumably Isaianic. See R. B. Y. Scott, *Interpr. Bible*, 5:278, and compare Otto Eissfeldt, *The Old Testament, an Introduction* (Oxford: Blackwell, 1965), p. 321. Compare the remark on Isa. 19:11 and Jer. 8:4 above, 4, o.

42. Against Hyatt, who omits 20:13 from his list of "confessional" material.

43. This adjective does not appear in Jer. again except in 30:12, 15.

44. So Rudolph, Jer.$_2$ p. 106, Jer.$_3$ p. 115; Mitchell Dahood, *Psalms I (Anchor Bible)*, p. 4, quoting C. A. Briggs, *Psalms (ICC)*, 1: 3, as "probably right."

45. So Dahood, *Psalms I*, p. 25.

46. The use of "heart" plus "fire" in 20:9 (cf. 17:1 and 4) seems fortuitous.

47. See 7, b, the third conclusion.

48. The verb *rpʾ* niphal appears in Jer. only otherwise in 19:11 (for which see below) and 51:8-9.

49. This root occurs otherwise in Jer. only in 50:9.

50. The word occurs otherwise in Jer. only in 7:6, 22:3, 49:11.

51. The word occurs otherwise in Jer. only in 49:9.

52. The word does not appear otherwise in Jer. (as already implied in chap. 4, n9).

53. These are the only two occurrences of this verb until chap. 22.

54. So Hyatt.

55. I note that *'attâ yāda'tā yhwh* occurs in 15:15 and *'attâ yāda'tā môṣā' śᵉpātay* in 17:16, but there are no other examples of the word order given.

56. For this suggestion see Hyatt.

57. Outside this passage, in the OT only in Deut. 5:3, 29:8, 13, 2 Ki. 23:3.

58. In v. 9, and not otherwise in Jer.; in the other prophets only in Isa. 8:12 twice (probably in the political sense) and Ezek. 22:25 (where the text is suspect); the noun is not found in Deut., nor the verb *qšr* in the sense of "conspire."

59. J. W. Miller, *Das Verhältnis Jeremias und Hesekiels Sprachlich und Theologisch Untersucht* (Assen, Holland: Van Gorcum, 1955), pp. 42-47, suggests that 11:1-8 is an echo of Deut. 27:14-26, while 11:9-14 corresponds to Deut. 16:17-19.

60. So Volz, Rudolph. Note that *rā'â* in the sense of "disaster" does not appear in chap. 7; the word appears only once there, 7:12, in the sense of "wickedness."

61. The word *bāśār* is not common in Jer., and has not appeared heretofore in the book; further occurrences through chap. 20 are 12:12, 17:5, 19:9.

62. Note what is stated below (chap. 9 [4]) on the hope complex, namely, that it is a self-sustaining unit beginning and ending with *geber* (30:6, 31:22); the new covenant passage is then an addition to the hope complex, linked by *ḥᵃdāšâ* (31:22, 31).

NOTES TO CHAPTER 9

1. Lundbom (see Intro., n18 above), pp. 31-32.
2. See my analysis in *JBL* 85 (1966): 424-32.
3. Lundbom (see Intro., n18 above), pp. 32-33.
4. This is the suggestion of Claus Rietzschel, *Das Problem der Urrolle* (Gütersloh: Gütersloher Verlagshaus, Gerd Mohn, 1966), p. 128. These are the only two occurrences of the word in Jer. as a direct object; there are two other occurrences as object of a preposition—8:18, 31:13.

NOTES TO CHAPTER 10

1. See chap. 6, n4.
2. See 4, p.

3. See a discussion of this matter in *JBL* 85 (1966): 401-35 *passim.*

4. The suggestion of Weiser.

5. So Rudolph.

6. The scholars whose views come closest to the one presented here are Rietzschel (the first scroll is Jer. 1-6, and the second scroll adds 7-20; pp. 130-31) and Hyatt (the second scroll contains most of the passages in 1:4-9:1; *Interpr. Bible* 5: 787). Rudolph's suggestion is quite different (see Intro. and Intro., n3), as is Eissfeldt's (see again Intro. and Intro., n4); Weiser and Bright do not attempt a specific solution.

Bibliography

Albright, William F. "The Refrain 'And God saw *kî ṭôb.*' " *Mélanges bibliques rédigés en l'honneur d'André Robert.* Paris: Bloud & Gay, 1957, pp. 2-26.

Bauernfeind, O. "*Trecho,*" in Kittel, R., ed., *Theological Dictionary of the New Testament*. Grand Rapids, Mich.: Wm. B. Eerdmans, 1964-1974, 8:226-35.

Baumgartner, Walther. *Hebräisches und Aramäisches Lexicon zum Alten Testament.* Leiden: E. J. Brill, 1967-

Beauchamp, Paul. "L'analyse structural et l'exégèse biblique." *Congress Volume, Supplements to Vetus Testamentum* 22. Leiden: E. J. Brill, 1972, pp. 113-28.

Berridge, John M. *Prophet, People, and Word of Yahweh, Basel Studies in Theology* 4. Zürich: EVZ-Verlag, 1970.

Braulik, Georg. "Aufbrechen von geprägten Wortverbindungen und Zusammenfassen von stereotypen Ausdrücken in der alttestamentlichen Kunstprosa." *Semitics* 1 (1970): 7-11.

Briggs, C. A. and E. G. *A Critical and Exegetical Commentary on the Book of Psalms*. New York: Scribner, 1906-7.

Bright, John. *Jeremiah, The Anchor Bible* 21. New York: Doubleday, 1965.

Condamin, Albert. *Le Livre de Jérémie, Études Bibliques.* Paris:

Gabalda, 1936.
Cornill, C. H. *Das Buch Jeremia.* Leipzig: Tauchnitz, 1905.
Culley, Robert C. "Some Comments on Structural Analysis and Biblical Studies." *Congress Volume, Supplements to Vetus Testamentum* 22. Leiden: E. J. Brill, 1972, pp. 129-42.
Dahood, Mitchell. "Two Textual Notes on Jeremiah." *Catholic Biblical Quarterly* 23 (1961): 462-6.
———. "Hebrew-Ugaritic Lexicography I." *Biblica* 44 (1963): 283-303.
———. *Psalms I, II, III. The Anchor Bible* 16, 17, 17A. New York: Doubleday, 1966-70.
———. "The Metaphor in Jeremiah 17,13." *Biblica* 48 (1967): 109-10.
Driver, G. R. "Two Misunderstood Passages of the Old Testament." *Journal of Theological Studies,* n.s. 6 (1955): 82-87.
Duhm, Bernhard. *Das Buch Jeremia. Kurzer Hand-Commentar zum Alten Testament* 11. Tübingen: J. C. B. Mohr, 1901.
Eissfeldt, Otto. *The Old Testament, An Introduction.* Oxford: Basil Blackwell, 1965.
Ewald, Heinrich. *Commentary on the Prophets of the Old Testament.* Translated by J. Frederick Smith. London: Williams & Norgate, 1875-80.
Freedman, David Noel. *Prolegomenon* to G. B. Gray, *The Forms of Hebrew Poetry.* New York: KTAV, 1972.
Gesenius, W. and Kautzsch, E., *Hebrew Grammar.* 2d Engl. ed. Edited by A. E. Cowley. Oxford: Clarendon Press, 1910.
Giesebrecht, F. *Das Buch Jeremia, Handkommentar zum Alten Testament.* Göttingen: Vandenhoeck & Ruprecht, 1907.
Good, Edwin M. "The Composition of Hosea." *Svensk Exegetisk Årsbok,* 31 (1966): 21-63.
Gordon, Cyrus. *Ugaritic Textbook.* Rome: Pontifical Biblical Institute, 1965.
Gray, John. *I & II Kings.* Philadelphia: Westminster Press, 1970.
Guillaume, Alfred. "Metallurgy in the Old Testament." *Palestine Exploration Quarterly* 94 (1962): 129-32.
Harris, Zellig. "Linguistic Structure of Hebrew." *Journal of the American Oriental Society* 61 (1941): 143-67.
Heschel, Abraham. *The Prophets.* New York: Harper, 1962.

Hobbs, T. R. "Some Remarks on the Structure and Composition of the Book of Jeremiah." *Catholic Biblical Quarterly* 34 (1972): 257-75.

Holladay, William L. "Prototype and Copies: A New Approach to the Poetry-Prose Problem in the Book of Jeremiah." *Journal of Biblical Literature* 79 (1960): 351-67.

———. "On Every High Hill and Under Every Green Tree." *Vetus Testamentum* 11 (1961): 170-76.

———. "The So-Called Deuteronomic Gloss in Jeremiah viii 19b." *Vetus Testamentum* 12 (1962): 494-98.

———. "The Background of Jeremiah's Self-Understanding: Moses, Samuel, and Psalm 22." *Journal of Biblical Literature* 83 (1964): 153-64.

———. "The Priests Scrape Out on their Hands, Jeremiah v 31." *Vetus Testamentum* 15 (1965): 111-13.

———. "Jeremiah and Moses, Further Considerations." *Journal of Biblical Literature* 85 (1966): 17-27.

———. "The Recovery of Poetic Passages of Jeremiah." *Journal of Biblical Literature* 85 (1966): 401-35.

———. Review of Claus Rietzschel, *Das Problem der Urrolle, Vetus Testamentum* 18 (1968): 400-405.

———. "Form and Word-Play in David's Lament over Saul and Jonathan." *Vetus Testamentum* 20 (1970): 153-89.

———. "The Covenant with the Patriarchs Overturned: Jeremiah's Intention in 'Terror on Every Side' (Jer. 20:1-6)." *Journal of Biblical Literature* 91 (1972): 305-20.

Hyatt, J. Philip. "The Book of Jeremiah, Introduction and Exegesis." *The Interpreter's Bible* 5. New York: Abingdon, 1956, pp. 777-1142.

Kessler, Martin. "From Drought to Exile, A Morphological Study of Jer. 14:1-15:4." *Proceedings of the Society of Biblical Literature* (1972), pp. 501-25.

Koehler, L. et Baumgartner, W. *Lexicon in Veteris Testamenti Libros*. Leiden: E. J. Brill, 1953.

Lane, Edward W. *Arabic-English Lexicon.* London: 1863-93.

Lord, Albert B. *The Singer of Tales, Harvard Studies in Comparative Literature* 24. 1960, reprinted by Atheneum Press, 1965.

Lundbom, Jack R. *Jeremiah: A Study in Ancient Hebrew Rhetoric.* Society of Biblical Literature and Scholars' Press, 1975.

McKay, J. W. "Man's love for God in Deuteronomy and the father/teacher—son/pupil relationship." *Vetus Testamentum* 72 (1972): 426-35.

Miller, J. W. *Das Verhältnis Jeremias und Hesekiels sprachlich und theologisch untersucht.* Assen, Holland: Van Gorcum, 1955.

Mowinckel, Sigmund. *Zur Komposition des Buches Jeremia.* Christiania, 1914.

Muilenburg, James. "A Study of Hebrew Rhetoric: Repetition and Style." *Supplements to Vetus Testamentum* 1. Leiden: E. J. Brill, 1953, pp. 97-111.

———. "Form Criticism and Beyond," *Journal of Biblical Literature,* 88 (1969): 1-18.

———. "Baruch the Scribe," in John I. Durham and J. Roy Porter, eds., *Proclamation and Presence, Old Testament Essays in Honour of Gwynne Henton Davies.* (Richmond, Va.: John Knox Press, 1970, pp. 215-38.

Overholt, Thomas W. "The Falsehood of Idolatry: An Interpretation of Jer. x 1-16." *Journal of Theological Studies,* n. s. 16 (1965): 1-12.

———. *The Threat of Falsehood, Studies in Biblical Theology.* 2d ser. 16. London: S.C.M. Press, 1970.

von Rad, Gerhard. *Wisdom in Israel.* New York: Abingdon, 1972.

Reventlow, Henning Graf. *Liturgie und prophetisches Ich bei Jeremia.* Gütersloh: Gütersloher Verlagshaus, Gerd Mohn, 1963.

Rietzschel, Claus. *Das Problem der Urrolle.* Gütersloh: Gütersloher Verlagshaus, Gerd Mohn, 1966.

Rudolph, Wilhelm. Critical apparatus to Jeremiah in *Biblia Hebraica, editio tertia.* Stuttgart: Privilegierte Württembergische Bibelanstalt, 1950.

———. *Jeremia, Handbuch zum Alten Testament* 12. Tübingen: J. C. B. Mohr, 2d ed. 1958, 3d ed. 1968.

———. Critical apparatus to Jeremiah in *Biblia Hebraica Stuttgartensia 8, Liber Jeremiae praeparavit W. Rudolph.* Stuttgart: Württembergische Bibelanstalt, 1970.

Scott, R. B. Y. "Isaiah 1-39, Introduction and Exegesis." *The Interpreter's Bible* 5. New York: Abingdon, 1956, pp. 151-381.

Skinner, John. *Prophecy and Religion.* Cambridge: Cambridge

University Press, 1922.

Soggin, J. Alberto. "Jeremias vi 27-30, Einige Textkritische Bemerkungen." *Vetus Testamentum* 9 (1959): 95-98.

———. "La 'Negazione' in Geremia 4, 27 e 5, 10a, cfr. 5, 18b." *Biblica* 46 (1965): 56-59.

Speiser, E. *Genesis, The Anchor Bible* 1. New York: Doubleday, 1964.

Volz, Paul. *Der Prophet Jeremia, Kommentar zum Alten Testament.* Leipzig: A. Deichertsche Verlagsbuchhandlung D. Werner Scholl, 1928.

Weinfeld, Moshe. *Deuteronomy and the Deuteronomic School.* London: Oxford University Press, 1972.

Weiser, Artur. *Das Buch Jeremia, Das Alte Testament Deutsch* 20/21. 6th ed. Göttingen: Vandenhoeck & Ruprecht, 1969.

Weiss, Meir. "Die Methode der 'Total-Interpretation.' " *Congress Volume, Supplements to Vetus Testamentum* 22. Leiden: E. J. Brill, 1972, pp. 88-112.

Wildberger, Hans. *Jesaja 1-12, Biblischer Kommentar, Altes Testament.* Neukirchen: Neukirchner Verlag, 1972.

Wolfe, R. E. "Introduction and Exegesis to Micah." *The Interpreter's Bible* 6. New York: Abingdon, 1956, pp. 897-949.

Index of Passages

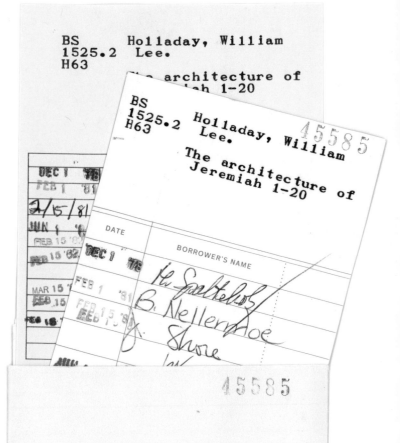